Parenting for Success

Parenting *for* Success

Raise Joyful, Fulfilled, *and* Effective Children

DANIEL KINGSTON
Family Success Institute

NEW YORK

LONDON • NASHVILLE • MELBOURNE • VANCOUVER

Parenting for Success

Raise Joyful, Fulfilled, and Effective Childre

Published in New York, New York, by Morgan James Publishing in partnership with Difference Press. Morgan James is a trademark of Morgan James, LLC.
www.MorganJamesPublishing.com

ISBN 9781642793987 paperback
ISBN 9781642793994 eBook
ISBN 9781642794007 audio
Library of Congress Control Number: 2018966357

Cover and Interior Design by:
Chris Treccani
www.3dogcreative.net

Morgan James is a proud partner of Habitat for Humanity Peninsula and Greater Williamsburg. Partners in building since 2006.

Get involved today! Visit
MorganJamesPublishing.com/giving-back

DEDICATION

For Paul, my parents, my family, and everyone else that makes a difference for families.

TABLE OF CONTENTS

FOREWORD

I have devoted my life and career to helping people access high performance. As a doctor, I do that through optimizing the brain and body of people around the world. And as a father of 3 boys, I'm looking for the best solutions to lead, organize and raise the family with excellence.

Daniel is one of the most remarkable people that I know. He is committed to growth and excellence in every aspect of his life – business, health, spiritual, financial, and of course, family. When he's committed to something, he won't stop until he has figured the best system out. When he was working with me, he completely transformed his health. Just like with his health, he's figured out some of the best systems for families to thrive.

After one health consultation he asked me, "How are things going on in your life?" I let him know that there were recent challenges raising my sons. I had read several parenting books, but I still couldn't understand how to get my sons to listen to me.

Working with executives, entrepreneurs, and various celebrities, I would think to myself, "I can get these world leaders to take control of their health and lives and get to the highest level of performance possible, and yet my kids are out of control!"

Daniel patiently and lovingly listened to me explain to him some of the situations I had dealt with. And then he opened his mouth. What proceeded was so profound and eye-opening that I asked him if he wouldn't mind relaying that message to my wife.

That evening, we received an email from him that was several paragraphs long. It was as if he had his PhD in parenting success.

Over the course of the weeks and months ahead, we flourished as parents. We implemented new systems in our home that had our children following through much more consistently with high levels of respect. What was the most profound thing of all, was the level of confidence that our kids developed. When you follow these systems in *Parenting for Success* you will not only have a more easier time parenting, but you will experience more joy and happiness while your children feel more love and grow more confidence.

Daniel comes from a true servant's heart and he cares deeply about families' success. I have known him for many years and he truly is committed to making a difference in his own family and in the lives of the people around him.

The techniques that Daniel teaches are the real thing. He also has a way of explaining that makes it simple to understand and easy to implement, if you follow his advice.

I know each family that works with him will reach a whole new level of joy and success in their family.

Enjoy this book. The investment you make in reading it will pay dividends for years to come. The ultimate dividend will come when you think of how great your family turned out in your last breaths on this earth.

Investing in becoming a successful parent is far more precious than silver and gold. Upgraded parents create upgraded parenting, which creates an upgrade in your children which creates an upgrade in the world. I believe that this book, if applied, will change the world.

To Successful Parenting Changing the World,

Dr. Isaac Jones

"Whatever is worth doing at all, is worth doing well."
– Philip Stanhope

I Thought This Was Going to Be Easier

I don't think anyone ever said being a parent was going to be easy. I don't think anyone *really* assumes it will be easy after they get started with their family. We, as parents, are not necessarily looking for easy either. The joys, fulfillment, and possibilities of having a family are so compelling that we are pretty sure we can handle it. Right?

It's true, being a parent is one of the most amazing and rewarding experiences we can possibly imagine and life's meanings become real and purposeful. Parents can also experience unbelievable uncertainty, heartache, pain, despair, regret, and sadness in their family. Some parents are extremely proactive and responsible and do their best to be great parents, realizing the power and impact that they have. Other parents act as if they are the victim of their circumstances and succumb to their environment and blame everything else around them for the condition their family is in. A lot of uncontrollable and unforeseen situations come up in the lives of our family. It takes so much effort to take seemingly simple steps. If constant effort isn't applied, the law of entropy kicks in with our family, relationships, and life.

Sometimes it seems like we are alone, completely alone. That no one understands what we are going through or worse, that no one cares. But we care. We care so much about our children. We care that they are getting everything they need to maximize the wonderful potential that maybe only we see in them. We care that they can avoid, or at least navigate, the challenges of life. Challenges that we've gone through. Challenges that we see or know others go through. Challenges that we know they are going to face. How do we do it? How can we include it all? Where in the world did my child come from? How do I handle all this?

Love is so extremely powerful. It can get us through it, sort of. It is at least the energy or fuel we need to carry forward or find the solution. But, it's still only based on our own knowledge and experience. Why is there not a required parenting curriculum that begins in grade school? Just like math or reading. For 4+ years, we are taught the basics in words and numbers. Then in late elementary and junior high, we are taught application and can begin solving real life problems with calculations or creating literary works.

And if we continue our studies, we can become master engineers, business professionals, or authors.

What about the basics of parenting? You could even describe it as the "basics of living life." Isn't *that* what we are actually teaching our children? How to live life? How to succeed at something? How to find something? How to create themselves and be the person they are meant to be? And we are not talking about small things here. We are not talking about a simple academic problem. We are talking about how to be successful in finding your soul mate. Or finding God. Or finding your purpose. Or finding out what it takes to accomplish something. We are talking about how to mentally and emotionally develop to handle very real and often serious problems in life. We are talking about how to succeed and what it looks like. We are talking about the practical efforts that make life work. We are talking about what principles or practices work and which ones don't.

We are talking about what life itself is and how to live it. How's that for a challenge?

Being a great parent is *the* most important job, role, profession (however you want to look at it) that we have. How do you do it successfully? How can we live life with our family and truly experience the joys of life and help these small people (our children) do the same thing? It's interesting how often it seems like the neighbors have it all figured out, or it doesn't seem to be as hard for someone else.

Do any of the following questions seem familiar to you? Why is my house always a mess when I'm a clean person? Or at least I used to be. Why is it such an epic battle to get my son into bed almost every single night? It seems like I give *everything* to my children, why don't they respect me or do what I tell them to? Why are our mornings so chaotic? Why aren't my kids doing well in school? How can I set up a fulfilling home life? Why does my teenager seem disconnected with our family?

One of the modern challenges that we have as parents is protecting our children with the global connectivity we have with the Internet. Most children literally must have Internet access to function in school and most other activities. Later, we will discuss character versus experience and what it looks like to handle all this connectivity. Nearly *all* communication is through a mobile device or computer that literally can access *any* type of information or subject that you can think of. How do we handle all this? It's hard enough just to make a living to pay the rent and put food on the table, let alone the time, effort, and energy to raise successful, happy children in this modern age.

I know a family that struggles to consistently get their kids to school on time *and* have them all eat a decent breakfast every day. Their mornings are chaotic and undisciplined. The real worry isn't necessarily the low citizenship grade from the tardiness but the habits and perspective the kids are creating from the morning experience as they grow up.

One of the reasons the last few generations have been having fewer children is because of the perception of some of the challenges we've talked about. There seems to also be a global push for a population decrease. Without getting into the population debate, I want to pose a few questions to you. What is important to you and your family? What is God's purpose for your life and family? What legacy do you want to leave when you are gone? What part of that legacy include your children? What type of family are you or do you want to be? People often have a sense of how many children they are meant to have, and if you have one or thirteen, the challenges and responsibilities are similar.

Here is another interesting question. How many children would you have if you knew you could handle it emotionally, financially, and practically? We sometimes feel limited or confined in even handling what we currently have, let alone the possibility for more. And the reasons for feeling limited might be easier to solve than you think. Each family needs to seriously think about these questions and carefully make decisions that are right for them. And no, it's not easy, but it's worth it. Which means it's easier to do it, than not.

Whatever you hope for your family, there are simple systems that can bring you happier days with them. You can raise joyful, fulfilled, and effective children without the struggle. Turn the page to learn how.

Chapter 1

My Story

"Don't let perfection get in the way of progress."
— Tony Bombacino

Growing Up

I am the oldest of thirteen children and was born when my parents were 20 years old (my father is two months older than my mother). I witnessed my parents raise an amazing family while taking on the challenges of life. Being an observant child, I paid attention to people and always asked the question, "Why do people do that?" I went to high school and watched young adolescents try to figure life, and themselves, out. And, like everyone else, I was trying to do the same thing myself. We didn't have the textbook either.

One of my best friends in high school had his backyard against the fence of the tennis courts across the street from the high school. My house was farther north, but not too far to enjoy a 20-minute walk each way. Often, I would take my bike instead and store it at my friend's house and we would both walk the last half block together. We met in elementary and became closer friends in middle school. We did everything together, at least as much as we could. He meant so much to me and I deeply cared about him.

A few years after I got married, I asked my friend if I could take him to lunch for his birthday. It had been a few months since we really spoke and we hadn't done anything together for about a year. He accepted, and we went to a restaurant to talk. He had moved out of his parents' house and had been going to college for about a year. He had changed. Although he was doing okay in college (not great), I could tell that he wasn't entirely interested in it and had no idea what he wanted to actually do with his life. All he knew is that he wanted to get away from his parents. During the meal, I tried to talk about things the way we used to. Having deep conversations about life and dreams and such. He kept the conversation fairly light and I finally called him out and asked what was going on. He simply told me, "I don't trust you." "Don't trust me? Don't trust me with what?" I thought. I was dumbfounded and shocked and didn't really know what to say. The stabbing pain in my throat made it harder to speak and try to salvage the connection any way that I could. I desperately felt the final blows of an already dwindling friendship in those few moments. We had been there for two hours and we both needed to leave soon. I gave him a ride back to his apartment and told him that if there is *anything* he needed to please let me know. Before that summer was over, he moved and didn't tell any of his family where he was going and I haven't heard anything from him since. That was over 20 years ago.

The pain was unbelievable. I went over in my mind a million times what could have happened. What went wrong? How could our lives go in such different directions? What could I have done different? What made the difference?

Life is hard enough dealing with *normal* challenges. How does someone handle the *hard* stuff? I had a small child of my own and I couldn't bear the thought of her growing up and hating her family or destroying her life. No child certainly starts out that way. By the time we had this lunch together, he was addicted to video games and had friends in college that would later get him on drugs.

What happened? That was the plaguing question I had for weeks. Then I realized, I know exactly what happened. I watched it unfold for years. In my young mind, I thought that our friendship would make up the difference, and I didn't realize that he spent *most* of his time at home. Our friendship was amazing and meaningful, but it was not enough to compensate for the belief structures, practices, and experiences of home.

His mother was "kind of" an alcoholic. I say "kind of" because she didn't always drink, and most of the time when she did, it was in pretty good moderation. However, there was never really a time over the years, where she wouldn't go too far in her drinking and then go too far in everything else. I would sometimes find my friend thrown out of his house and just sitting on the lawn. He was too embarrassed or ashamed to take my offer to come to my house. He would just say that he got thrown out again without much of an explanation. Sometimes he would open up and talk about when his mother would get violent and throw dishes at the kids and scream about everything. Often for him, home life depended on what mood she was in. If she was in a good mood, everything was great, even too complacent, and the kids could do whatever they wanted. It didn't matter if they did something wrong when she was in a good mood, since she would just laugh it off. If they did something good, when she was in a good mood, she would smile and not make it that big a deal of it either.

When his Mom was in a bad mood, nothing was good. Everything was wrong, and the kids paid the price. Punishment was severe when they did something wrong and nothing was good enough when they tried to do something right. His once tender heart and infectious smile turned to hate and bitterness, and it didn't have to be that way.

This had a deep and profound impact on me.

I looked around and could see *everyone* has challenges in parenting to one degree or another. How do I not screw up my own kids? What are we all going to do? I began studying and collecting parenting material everywhere that I could. I started asking parents for interviews about their successes and failures in their families. Most people were more than willing to give a young father parenting advice. A lot of things were contradictory at times and I began focusing on the very specific patterns and principles that made it work. I also focused on things that had a track record of results.

As we began implementing and putting what we learned into practice, people started noticing a difference with our children. They were consistently getting awards at school. Awards like Student of the Month or Student of the Year. We had children competing in swimming. We had our oldest in college and doing very well. Back when our oldest son was just eleven years old, he got a couple of his young brothers together and wrote a Brothers Mission Statement on his own, portions of which I'll include here:

Brothers Mission Statement

"We, the brothers of the …….. family will promise with all our hearts to love, care, watch out for, teach, help, respect, work, succeed, accomplish, live, obey, acknowledge, understand and be honest to each other in perfect harmony, charity, friendship, and the Spirit of the Lord.

We will watch out, pay attention to, and respect the feelings, thoughts, and actions of each other. We will treat others around us as we would want them to treat us. We…. know we were given some of the greatest blessings of all.

…

We … work together in doing what's right. We are very best friends and play, work, and help each other lovingly.

….

We will forever be brothers, partners, and friends, …. together in PEACE and LOVE."

I was shocked and touched when I first read this. This is just an example of what is possible if you can line up things in your home the way it needs to be.

We still have challenges like everyone else. Even though it's not easy, it is extremely rewarding to succeed in what matters most. There are many important parts to actually make it all work. In the next chapter, I will discuss some critical foundational things that are important to understand as you begin to establish your routines and assessments.

CHAPTER 2:

Establishing a Foundation

"Little by little, a little becomes a lot."
– TANZANIAN PROVERB

The Words That Come out of Our Mouth

Even at the very beginning of infancy, our children "hear" us through the words that we speak. But, it's not just the words. In fact, our tonality and expression are stronger throughout our child's life than words. Saying the words "I love you" in an angry or mocking tone versus in a loving or caring tone sends a completely different message to our infants and our teenagers. So, the real communication is the tone, expression, and presence as we speak.

I was observing a parent, watching her speak and interact with her children as they were getting ready for dinner. They were gathering the dishes to set on the table as well as putting the cooked food in serving dishes. They had about five children to gather and there was a fair amount of activity to accomplish all this. When she turned and spoke to me, she had a much softer tone than she did while speaking to her children. She didn't realize that she changed her tone that much and I told her that I would like her to audio-record herself during the dinner hour with her children.

It took a while before she got around to doing it, but when she did, she was shocked. Even with the awareness of the recorder going, she was surprised how harsh she sounded when she was interacting with her children. She immediately became more present to the communication she was having with her children. She realized that her children's self-image was largely due to *how* she spoke with as well as *what* she said.

Children are always gauging love from those around them. They judge (usually unconsciously) the level that someone might love them. They are also deciding how to act in the situation themselves. When this mother simply changed her tone, spoke softer and more slowly, her children felt a deeper connection to her. She always loved them. But, they heard it to a much greater degree when she changed her tone.

This is an exercise I highly recommend to all my clients. Often, we hear the internal dialog and our intentions when we speak and not the tone and words that are actually coming out of our mouths. Being present to what we are saying and how we are saying it will help us understand how other people are experiencing us and offer the opportunity for us to change it for the better.

Another important aspect is to "Say what you mean, and mean what you say." Choose your words extremely carefully. So often we casually say things that we don't mean at all or that are not true. Our children learn very fast. If we carelessly say things that aren't true – like we are going to do something when we really don't mean it or have no intention of actually doing it – we show them not only how to lie, but that it's okay to lie. Even if it seems innocent or small, small things grow to big things, especially as our children grow and have more complex lives.

An important exercise is to bring your presence and awareness to the words, tone, and expression of your communication with your children. An audio recording is very helpful to hear how you are coming across (as mentioned earlier) and is highly recommended. The actual words are also critical and that you say things that are actually possible when you tell your child to do something. For example, a parent might be shopping and her child is being noisy or is climbing all over the grocery cart. I can't count how many times I've heard things like "Be Quiet," or "Sit Still," come from parents. Think about that for just a minute. What do we actually mean when we say things like that? Do we really expect our two-year-old child to sit completely still or be totally quiet? It doesn't take long to realize that they are both quite impossible to actually comply with. And now we have a bigger problem on our hands. We have to either enforce something that is not possible or train the child that what we say doesn't matter or doesn't make sense.

Instead of being careless with our words, we need to say what we mean (really) and mean what we say (really). For example, we could say, "That's too loud in the store, you need to be more quiet." And then demonstrate what "more" quiet means by either your own soft-spoken words or maybe a whisper and help them get there. Or instead of "sit still," we can say, "You have to sit in the basket and you can't climb around the cart." Be wise, as a parent, of your child's ability to comply with what you are telling them to do and don't tell them to do something they can't.

Authority and Discipline

Depending on who you ask, or what TV show you watch, the words "authority" and "discipline" sometimes have a negative connotation to them in today's society. I view respect for authority and the idea of discipline as, quite literally, some of the greatest gifts we can give ourselves and our children. Let's think about it for just a minute. Because we respect authority, we are granted the gift of safety when we drive our vehicles on the roads with thousands of other drivers by following the traffic laws. Authority makes it possible for many people to function in a society without each person having to worry about and take care of literally everything. The police and judicial system take care of enforcing laws. The municipalities take care of roads and infrastructure. The power company runs power lines that connect directly to my house and all I have to do is be in compliance and pay my power bill. With zero authority, society would not exist in any organized state and we could not survive very long. Teaching children authority teaches them to value other people and value themselves because that authority has impact and can create results.

Teaching children to share is a form of teaching respect for authority. It also helps them to respect themselves as well as others. When a child owns a toy, they have authority over that toy. It belongs to them. When we teach a child to politely ask to play with someone else's toy, they are respecting the authority that someone else has over the toy they want to play with. We teach our children that when we go to someone else's house, we respect the rules that person has for their house. Maybe they take off their shoes to go in the living room, etc.

It's important for parents to understand and own that they are the authority for their children. Children need to understand that and act accordingly to be able to grow into happy and productive adults. Teaching respect for authority grants our children the gift of possibility to have literally endless options in life and also to have a meaningful relationship with the ultimate authority, God.

We can all use more discipline, right? When we have discipline, we are committed to consistently doing something that gets a certain result. How do we actually get discipline? It mostly comes from either the rewards (intrinsic or extrinsic) or the pain (intrinsic or extrinsic) of doing something or not doing something, doesn't it? We condition our minds to perform and we do it, often when we don't feel like it, but we use the intrinsic or extrinsic rewards or pain to do it anyway. When we *discipline* our children, we are guiding them to a specific result or direction because often, we can see the impact of what they are doing or not doing and know what needs to be different. Success comes from good habits and results come from taking action. And whatever habits *you* have (good or bad) will likely be passed on to your children. The reward (result) is always worth the effort. Use the result you're after to motivate yourself in the moment. Our child is literally in our training as we teach them how to be and what to do that will be best for them in life. It takes quite a long time for our young human brain to understand consequences and be able to make effective decisions. Just watch any teenager. I recommend you read the book "Dare to Discipline" by Dr. James Dobson to understand specific techniques and ideas that will help in the area of discipline, especially for smaller children.

Discipline of children needs to be in consequences that matter to them. Consequential thinking is an important aspect of a child's development. If the effect, or result we are after, is missing in our life or our children's lives, so is the cause of that result. Discipline and consequences help guide and train them to set up the cause so they can get the effect they are after.

I was working with a mother with a small three-year-old, energetic boy that barely listened to anything she would say, let alone actually *doing* what she said. We talked about the importance of him understanding that mommy is in charge and gets to decide what things he can play with in the house. We described that his toys are *his* and the books in the living room are mommy's and he can't get them without mommy helping and getting them for him.

Of course, at first, the simple explanation was not enough. Here is what we did. I picked up one of his toys and crouched down to his level and described how this toy is his and how he can play with it and how fun it is. Then I took him over to the mommy's books and showed him that he can't even touch those books without mommy first getting them and sitting with him to look at them. I showed him how to ask mommy. "Mommy, can I please look at those books?" and then he needed to wait for her to get them for him. I also walked him over to the chair next to the wall that he would sit on if he got into mommy's things without asking her first.

Do you think he then changed his behavior? Of course not, not yet anyway. I watched extremely close, and when he did get the books he wasn't supposed to, I walked over to him and explained *everything* again. His ownership, mommy's ownership, his responsibility, and the consequence. Only this time I said, "Now you have to go sit on the chair," and gently took his hand and walked him over. You might wonder, "How do you get an energetic three-year-old to sit on a chair as a consequence?" The first few times, I sat with him. I simply sat on the chair and put him on my lap and showed him how we need to sit on the chair. We don't talk (I would explain things in a whisper). We don't play. We just sit quietly for five minutes. Then when five minutes were over, I would speak energetically again and walk back over to the bookshelf and explain everything *again*. I continued to watch and follow up on the training as needed, doing the best that I could to not let him get away with it once the expectation was set. Fairly quickly, he caught on and understood what was expected. As his mother watched the training, she began applying it to other things she would have him do. He changed into a *happy,* energetic, three-year-old that understands ownership and has the beginnings of respect of others.

The techniques and strategies you will learn in this book will set up a condition where your children will have earned different freedoms. If our children can receive a reward after they have worked for it, it trains their brain to put forth effort to get a result. Those results can be freedoms, bonus time, or other rewards. There is a very satisfying feeling of earning free time on an activity. Value is perceived as something that is earned, worked for, paid for, or takes effort or resources to create. Appreciation comes from a perception of value. Gratitude comes with perceiving and enjoying something of value. Without appreciation and gratitude, our children can grow to be quite miserable. Even with a good intentioned parent. A child that is always given everything without earning it develops a distorted sense of value and a lack of appreciation. They become entitled and self-centered, always trying to satisfy an empty need that will never be fulfilled.

We can have gratitude for something we didn't necessarily earn, such as a sunset, because we appreciate and value the beauty, or the complexity, or the wonder, or the Creator of the sunset. We teach appreciation and gratitude by teaching value and care, and valuable meanings of things. As parents, we need to often communicate the value of things and the value of the people around us to our children.

Come Tell Me When You Are Done

One technique that helps create a strong tie with parents and children is to have your child "come tell you when they are done" after you tell them to do something. You don't have to do this every time, but when you do, make it count. For example, when you hand your 4-year-old child a folded pair of socks and go tell them to, "Go put them in your dresser," and say, "Come back and tell me when you are done," it opens up a great opportunity for a lot of things: First, it gives you a chance to see their level of obedience and if they will hurry and do it when you asked. It also lets them *prove* to you their level of obedience and gives them a chance to demonstrate it. You can train any improvements in obedience as needed.

Second, it gives you a chance to show them that you are pleased with them and their performance at something. You should make it a big deal with a smile, a hug, a high-five, and lots of encouraging praise of their performance how fast they did it, how careful they were, how much you loved their attitude, how much you loved them taking care of their socks, how much you appreciate them contributing to the house, etc.

Third, it gets them used to communicating with you. Parents need to continually communicate and set up opportunities to connect with their children as they grow up. Creating opportunities of positive communication during work or achieving something (not just during play) is very valuable to your children.

The Eight-Minute Rule

Have you ever had the (not so) pleasure of being the parent that comes to tell your nine-year-old that it's time for bed or to come to dinner during his epic Lego battle of the Avengers versus the Aliens? Or that it's time to come in the house in the middle of their exploring expedition in the backyard? If you have, you know there are a few issues you could likely deal with. One, he may protest and complain and ask or demand that he is not done with destroying the alien base and needs more time. Or two, he says "OK," or "Just a minute," and it becomes your own epic battle of getting him to actually come to dinner. Or three, it causes some other disconnect or damage to the relationship from some other escalation. Or four, he just comes immediately the first time, with a smile. If he does, you need to clone him and pass one out to all the rest of us.

When our children are deeply engaged in an activity, many times it takes a little bit of time to unplug and refocus on something else. Some children can do this easier than others. If we are training obedience, we still can't allow this to be an excuse for disobedience because they will quickly learn how to manipulate the situation if we let them. What do we do then?

The answer is the eight-minute rule. Instead of coming in the room and telling them to come to dinner and either not really mean it (training disobedience or disregard for what we say) or abruptly interrupting (that may be difficult for them to transition), you simply say "In about eight minutes, I want you to come to dinner so you have about eight more minutes to play." This does a couple of things. It helps your child begin the transition from playing to not playing and coming to dinner. It also sets a future expectation for them to prepare for. It also gives them planned structure, even if it is only eight minutes in the future.

Notice that I said, "about eight minutes." That's because there is nothing special about eight minutes other than it is relatively soon. It could be five minutes. It could be ten minutes. I wouldn't make it much longer than 15 minutes because then the transition in the child's mind begins to stall and he re-engages in his activity again. It doesn't have to be precise either, as long as you say "about." Remember the idea of say what you mean and mean what you say? You say, "about eight minutes" and you might come back in seven minutes or ten minutes and tell him "Okay, it's now time to come to dinner." At this point, you can fully expect complete compliance. He knew it was coming and has been preparing for the transition. This works amazingly well for teenagers and even adults.

The Interrupt Rule

There is a lot going on in the young minds of children and often they want to come and tell us all about it. How do we, as parents, teach respect and keep a strong connection to what's going on in their world, all at the same time?

The interrupt rule is a powerful technique to do this. I was first introduced to this idea from a program written by Gary and Anne Marie Ezzo. The interrupt rule is that whenever Mom or Dad are talking or their attention is on something else, and the child wants to tell them something, the child places her hand on the arm, leg, or shoulder of the parent in silence. The parent then acknowledges them by either briefing looking at them, smiling, or placing their own hand on the child's hand (even without looking at them). Then, when the parent is ready to give the child attention, they look at them and listen to what they have to say. If the parent is talking to someone else, for example, the child can come over and put their hand on Mom and Mom can then put her own hand on top to acknowledge that she knows she is there and will give the child attention when she is finished talking or ready.

The parent can teach this technique to pretty small children and have great results. This teaches the child respect for the parent and what they are doing, and it also can teach respect for others that are talking to Mom or Dad. When the child does demonstrate the interrupt rule, it's important for the parent to acknowledge them and tell them they appreciate them practicing the rule. It's also important to train them that in any kind of emergency, it's OK to just interrupt you no matter what you are doing.

Yes, Mom (or Dad)

Another wonderful technique I learned from the Ezzos was "Yes, Mom." Whenever you ask your child to do something or inform them of something, you immediately have your child say "Yes, Mom" or "Yes, Dad" back to you. This does several things: One, it shows that there is (at least partly) a listening connection between Mom and the child. Two, it is a verbal affirmative or agreement that they will comply with the instruction. And three, it triggers their minds to begin executing the instruction that was given and helps train first-time obedience.

It is amazing what this habit will do for your children. It also helps us parents be more conscious of our expectations and what we are telling our children. It is also helpful sometimes if we crouch or kneel down, so we can literally be face-to-face with our children when they say, "Yes, Mom." At the very least, have them look at you in the face when they say it. This creates a powerful connection and a very clear expectation. In training, it simply goes something like this: "It's now time to come into dinner … say, 'Yes, Mom.'" And you wait for your child to look up and say, "Yes, Mom." Then expect the child to begin to comply and come in to dinner. If they don't, then there is an additional obedience problem that needs to be addressed.

Once you have established some of these techniques and habits in your home, you will have a better foundation to be able to move forward in setting up you home for success. The next thing is understanding where you are going and creating your vision.

CHAPTER 3:

Mission and Vision

"What is not started will never get finished."
– JOHANN WOLFGANG VON GOETHE

Vision Versus Specifics

There are three broad steps to accomplishing and creating anything in life. Step 1: Understand and define the vision and mission to go along with it. Step 2: Identify the processes and routines needed to accomplish that mission and vision. Step 3: Identify and assign the people (maybe yourself) to run and execute those processes and routines to accomplish the vision in Step 1.

One of the most important ideas to understand in parenting (or in any role or goal) is vision. Vision is a term that is used to mean many different things and I want to describe what it means to me, especially as it applies to helping your kids succeed. Your vision is how you see your outcomes to be. It's more than just goals or accomplishments. It includes how things actually are in your family. Things like the mood or state of the people in your family. It includes the visual state of things, the routines that are happening, the aspirations, the targets, and the actual results you see your family reaching. It includes your faith, your connection with God, your outcomes of your life or children's lives, the type of people you want to be, and all the other big stuff you can think of.

I need to explain a principle idea that will help you understand what kind of vision I'm talking about. Imagine if you would, a straight vertical line with the word "Vision" at the top and the word "Specifics" at the bottom. Imagine this line to be a sliding range where the higher you go up the line, the more high-chunked or abstract your vision-result is and the lower you go, the more specific your vision-result is. Vision-results are outcomes or results that tie to your vision.

You can watch people communicate and you can notice if they are communicating with more high-level ideas and abstractions or if they are very specific or more detailed in what they are saying, or if they are somewhere in between. Often people miscommunicate with each other simply because they are trying to connect at different points along this vertical scale. You will also notice that when communication actually *does* happen, it is usually because one of them has moved their own communication along this scale to more closely match the other person, thus they begin to connect with abstract ideas or the specific details. This awareness is extremely powerful in your own communication and you can try it out.

If you have a very specific outcome like: "I want you to take out all the trash in the house to the garbage can and put the garbage can on the street Wednesday night," versus a more abstract outcome like: "I want you to take care of the trash," you often get very different results. Either vision-result can get what you are after. It just requires an awareness of your intentions, the person's understanding, ability to perform, and if they have already done it before.

Two more critical points about the vision and specific scale: 1. Reality lives on the specific end and specific behaviors create that reality. The specific usually requires greater clarity (which is good) and helps you actually make real progress. 2. You must start with vision or the upper end of the spectrum. Vision gives direction, guidance, and purpose. To not get lost in the weeds of the specific, you must have an overall mission and vision that includes large global ideals and principles that act as guides. You also need big goals or aspirations as a family to give guidance to your specific outcomes that you set.

Again, vision-results are the outcomes that tie to your vision. They can be large and abstract (toward the upper end of the scale) or very specific and measurable (toward the lower end of the scale). You need both types. And the clearer you can be, the better your results will be.

Think about examples where you were communicating (even to yourself) on the two ends of the spectrum and how each got you where you needed to be. Good business leaders spend energy on both ends of the spectrum but tend to be more on the vision side. Good engineers also spend energy on both ends of the spectrum but tend to be more on the specific side. You will notice your own children will have a tendency toward one end or the other. You as the parent must keep the vision of the family and help your children reach that vision by effectively communicating with them. This is especially true for teenagers. Often, simply communicating the vision of the family and who we are is enough to create a deep connection with your teenager and help him/her align with that vision in what they are doing. This is also a part of creating a family identity which we will go over in more detail later in the book.

Another important thing to notice is drama lives in the abstract. Abstract problems are unsolvable and unclear. Bringing some reality and getting into the specifics is how we solve problems. You'll also notice if it seems like not a lot of things are making progress or moving forward, it's likely because there is too much time being spent in the vision and not enough time on the ground (specifics) getting things done. Notice this about yourself and your children.

Character Versus Experience

A critical awareness of all parents in raising their children is the reality of their child's character versus their experience. And if you can keep their character ahead of their experience, along with a compelling vision, you are 90% there. That's it, I'm done. That's all you have to do. Just go do that. Well, if it were only that easy.

Let's talk about the extreme on both sides. Some parents will completely open up their children's exposure to everything. They will let them experience everything and be completely free with what they watch on TV, what social media they have access to, internet devices, friends, etc. Sometimes, the parents hold the idea that their children need to get out and experience the world as soon and as fast as possible so they can learn and grow.

Many parents see the problem with this approach. As soon as they experience something they are not ready for, they can get into serious, and often permanent, trouble. On the other extreme, some parents will completely shelter their child and not let them experience anything or at least to the degree they can possibly control. They avoid as much influence or exposure to their children that they can. Again, most parents can see the problems this can create of an underdeveloped child or a child that ends up rebelling anyway.

So, what is the answer? Well, if the answer is somewhere in the middle, how do you know where?

The answer is to keep the character ahead of the experience. And, if they do have an experience they don't know how to handle the right way, quickly train their character to be able to handle it. This often requires a lean toward the sheltered side while you proactively train their character. The exact point on the spectrum is different for different children, even in the same family. You have to be pretty aware and observant of what your child's character is like.

I appreciate very much that I don't smoke. It's not something I had to try and figure out if I wanted to or not, either. I have never tried a cigarette and I never will. That's just something that is not a part of who I am. In my first year of high school, a friend of my best friend came with us one time to my friend's house after school. We were all talking in the backyard and this other friend (Tony) pulled out some cigarettes and lit one up. He offered it to both of us to just try. Neither one of us smoked and my friend told me to just try it. "It doesn't mean that you will smoke your whole life, just try it," he said. I calmly and confidently refused and there wasn't any amount of pressure that would change my mind. Before that moment, my character around smoking was determined and already set that I would never smoke. When the experience presented itself, I could make the decision that was aligned with that character and who I wanted to be. I give credit to my parents in the pre-emptive training I had around smoking.

Society offers a lot of experiences to young children and parents have to be very careful and diligent in protecting their children's character and heart and in preparing them to face life in the best way. A lot of parents relax the training of their young children and wonder what happened when they become teenagers and seem to make poor choices. If they make poor choices when they are young and their character is not developed, they will make poor choices when they are older. It's not just hormones. It's primarily the character they have and how it's been developed up to that point.

Responsibility

One of the most valuable traits that can be taught to your (even young) child is responsibility. Some may think that this isn't realistic or practical, or that the child will miss out on being a kid somehow if they have responsibility. Most parents, however, know the value of responsibility and the well-being of their child. The system you are learning in this book is teaching responsibility to your children and will be invaluable to them throughout their entire life.

Responsibility also gives ownership and identity to the family of the child. In contrast, if a child is not responsible to contribute to the family in any way, that same child will have difficulty in staying close to the family, especially as a teenager. Family responsibility is vital in the child's development and this needs to start at a young age to be the most effective. When teaching responsibility, it's helpful to not be too vague and to be clear on the specific outcomes they are responsible for. Those outcomes might be tasks or just an understanding of an expectation they are responsible to reach. Responsibility also give ownership of the results. A child feels a sense of ownership for the things they are responsible for begins to prepare them to greater responsibilities as they mature.

Having Your Child's Heart

Another vitally critical element of parenting is having your child's heart. This means a few things. Your child feels they can trust you and feels trusted by you. You both have a high level of appreciation for each other. There is mutual love and respect for each other and there are clear expectations. The ways to get there are all throughout this book and beyond including many other great resources that will help bring about these conditions. I will outline a few of them here.

1. Love is a decision. Some people, especially children, might be a little confused on what love actually is. The media and modern entertainment would have us believe that love is only a feeling that we have inside about someone or something. The problem with this limited view of love is that it tends to be self-seeking or self-centered, and as a person judges if they have love or not, or if they are being loved or not, they tend to base it on what they feel in the moment. True love is not self-seeking, but self-sacrificing for the well-being of someone or something else. True love is a decision to act in a way that serves, uplifts, supports, and magnifies someone else. I believe the wisdom of God in having human babies be quite helpless at birth is, in part, to help us parents practice the *act* of love. We are also very blessed in the joy we find in loving our children, and loving does, in fact, come with a wonderful feeling. Notice in yourself how you love. And what specifically you feel and *do* when you are in love.

2. Create clear and consistent expectations that your children can understand. If a parent constantly changes their expectations of performance or standards with their children, they tend to lose trust. What is going to set Mom off this time? What

is actually going to happen? Clear expectations also help to make clear decisions. Clear expectations and decisions create a path or plan that will guide your child and family in the direction they need to go. The system I'm outlining in this book is going to make it easy to set expectations for your children in a way that makes sense.

3. Children need to be physically nurtured and loved. This can be hugs, kisses on the cheek, sitting close to Mom or Dad, holding hands to cross the street, being tucked into bed, being tickled, etc. This strengthens the unconscious bond your child has with you, especially young children. Their physical development is also closely linked to their neurological and emotional development.

4. Show respect to your children. One way of doing this is by *always* keeping your cool and treating them with respect. It makes it much easier to expect the same from them. Children will tend to treat people how you treat them, or how they see you treat people, not just how you tell them to treat people.

5. Tell your children "hello" when you arrive and "goodbye" when you leave. This shows a level

of love and respect and gives them a sense of certainty. Whenever I leave the house, I tell my wife "goodbye" and where I am going (usually) and I go around the house telling each child I am leaving and give them a hug and kiss. When I arrive, I go around and find the kids to tell them I'm home and give them another hug. I also teach the kids to do the same thing. They tell me or Mom before they go anywhere and they tell us they've arrived when they get home. This does many things. It creates an opportunity for the child to communicate where they are going and what they are doing. It also creates an unconscious trust and certainty that Mom or Dad are close by and communicating with them. It also demonstrates love and affection to the children as Mom and Dad show interest in what's going on in their world.

6. Encourage your children more than just praising them. Your child's young (and even your) unconscious mind is like a "little boy" or "little girl" inside. That little boy or little girl is highly moral and wants to make the right or best decision it can and also has an identity. Sometimes that identity is positive or negative in different aspects of that person's perception of themselves. To help shape a positive identity and reward, thus

encourage the behavior you want, you can frame your compliment something like this:

"You are (*talking to the unconscious mind*) very loving (*character trait that ties to identity*) and the reason I know this is because you came home and helped your little brother with his homework today (*encourage the action taken that you want repeated along with the identity of the character trait*)."

Without the reference to the action taken, it could just be empty praise. It's not going to permanently damage your child to just tell them once in while a trait they have with no reference tied to it. However, if that's all you do, then it can lead to confusion in your child if they happen to disagree with your compliment or they find themselves trying to measure up to an unknown expectation of an undefined ideal. Your child could also develop a blind identity where they think they are something different than the results their actions are getting them. Results come from actions. True self-esteem comes from what we *do*, not just what we think we are. Often the problem with teenagers not having self-esteem is they are trying to get it from thinking only. Have them start *doing* something meaningful or have them starte serving someone else to help them develop love and self-esteem.

As your child talks to themselves, you would encourage this type of self-dialog:

> "One great thing about me is I am (*unconscious mind talking to itself*) kind (*character trait*) and the reason I know this is because I helped my little brother with his homework after school today (*encouragement and action I did that should be repeated*)"

Create and communicate a compelling future for your children. Help your children be excited for things in life. As they grow, help them look forward to doing well in school, or learning new things, or taking on a hobby, experiencing new dynamics in the family (such as a new baby) or whatever is going on. Or even waking up in the morning. Help them appreciate the time they have with Mom, Dad, grandparents, or each other. Help them see the good in people and how they can become more by working hard. Obviously, you must be aware of their physical, mental, and emotional capacity to do things. Create a future of possibility for them in each area of life: spiritual, family, academic, physical, financial, career, etc. As stated before, be careful of keeping their character above their experience and participate with them in the steps they take in life.

Goals

There are a countless number of books, blogs, and references on goals and how to set goals. One guideline is to make goals SMART, which means Specific, Measurable, Actionable, Realistic, and Time-based (having a deadline). Goals are important; however, there are certain aspects of goals that are *more* important. Whenever I think of goals, I think of three types:

1. Achievement Goals: SMART goals that are clear, measurable, actionable, with a clear deadline are achievement goals. Most people that understand goals well set achievement goals. The best ones have measurable milestones and specific steps of achieving them. One such SMART achievement goal might be: "I want to lose 20 pounds in three months." And some steps to achieve it may be things like "stop eating sugar," "cut back on bread," "eliminate soda pop," "exercise four times a week," and so on. It's important to understand the other two types to best set and achieve these types of goals.

2. Habits: In order to accomplish an achievement goal of losing 20 pounds in three months, I have to consistently *do* something (create a habit) to achieve it. I will get to my goals much faster if I can

clearly identify the consistent behaviors that need to happen in order to achieve it. Habits are formed by repetitive action with energy. High emotional energy added during the action can create a habit faster.

3. Standards: This is most the important of the three types. Most people worry about setting and achieving goals, but don't set any standards. If habits are the *consistent* execution of something, standards are the *level* of execution. In order to accomplish a goal of losing 20 pounds in three months, I need to set standards of diet and exercise along with habits of consistently doing them to achieve the result. Setting a standard can happen immediately. Setting a standard with high emotional energy or leverage can forge a standard to last a very long time. It can last a lifetime, if it's reinforced and supported.

Think about your own goals and ask yourself what type they are: Achievement, Habits, or Standards. Achievement goals need to be SMART. Habits need to have the support of consistent execution and scheduling. And standards need to have a clear level of execution defined.

CHAPTER 4:

Processes and Routines

"Success is the sum of small efforts,
repeated day in and day out."
– R. COLLIER

Processes and Routines That Matter

Once you have the vision, mission, thinking systems, and some useful strategies, next, you need to create the processes and routines to accomplish that vision. When it comes to raising your children or setting up your home to be a place where a happy, healthy family thrives, what happens in your daily life creates it. Life is every day. Processes and routines are where the rubber meets the road and something magical actually begins to happen.

There are three main critical routines happening in every home (even if it's not how you want it): One, the morning routine. This is the time from when everyone wakes up to the time they are at school or work in the morning. If everyone is staying home, such as young children or home-schooled children, this is the time from when they wake up to the time they begin normal daytime activities (breakfast is included in the morning routine). Two, the afternoon or afterschool routine (which we will cover in the next chapter). And Three, the bedtime routine, which is obviously the time from when Mom or Dad says, "It's time to get ready for bed," (review the eight-minute rule) to the time the kids (not necessarily Mom or Dad) are in their beds asleep.

The Morning Routine

The morning, of course, sets the tone for the rest of the day. We often don't realize how big of an impact it really has. Our children watch us very carefully in everything we do. What do *we* do or say when *we* get up? Do *we* wake up happy? Do *we* act excited to meet the day? Making sure we greet the morning on a positive note is probably the most important place to start.

One of the wonderful gifts we can give our children is a bright smiling face (our own) that greets them into the new day. If we walk into our child's bedroom in the morning and wake them up (especially when they are young) with a gentle and excited voice "Good morning … it's time to get up … it's a beautiful day today … today is going to be a great day ... we are going to do <insert here> today," etc., it not only starts them off in a positive way, but pre-frames how their whole day can go.

Now, this is assuming they've gotten enough sleep, which we'll cover in the bedtime routine, and that they've had a comfortable night. Of course, not every morning will be like this, but not to worry, making this a consistent effort will get you amazing results.

Once the kids are awake, it's like being the director of a new play on opening night. And you have just moments to set in motion the performance of the household for the next hour or so before someone must go to school, work, or get ready for something else that day. So, what do you do? I want to outline a few ideas and principles that are extremely helpful and then offer some very specific ways to execute on those ideas that people have done.

There are Seven Gs of a Great Morning. You can change around the order that works best for you in your actual schedule. They are: God, Gratitude, Grounding, Growing, Goals, Good Food, and Go! This applies to you personally and to your children in the household. I will include a sample schedule for the household and for an individual.

God: This includes prayer and your connection to God. Family prayer is also an important thing to include in your mornings.

Gratitude: Think of, or journal, what you are grateful for in your life. Express five things you are grateful for to your children. Or, go into some detail of why you are grateful for just one thing. Have your children also express what they are grateful for. You can all talk about one theme each morning if you like.

Grounding: This includes some type of meditation, affirmations, or declarations. Set up your day to start from a centered place. There are many different practices and many benefits for including them in your morning. They don't have to be very long, either. Good music is also a great way to start the day in a positive trajectory.

Growing: Begin your day with some positive intellectual stimulation. You can read your book for ten minutes or watch a few minutes of a video lesson of the course you're taking, or even read scriptures with your kids. Something that stimulates learning and thinking.

Goals: Review (or create) your plan for the day and what you want to accomplish. As the kids get older, they can also use a simple notebook or planner system to plan their day. A day that is planned for is a day that is cared for.

Good Food: This should really be good nutrition, and it does *not* include sugar in a bowl. Breakfast cereal in a box is one of the worst things you can do to start your child's day nutritionally. There is countless evidence, references, and resources of what type of diet should be included in your family for optimal health. Read *The Case*

Against Sugar by Gary Taubes just as a start. Stick to basics and natural. Have a quality protein, quality plant-based carbohydrate (donuts don't count), and quality fats. Of course, talk to your health care professional for help in making the best nutritional decisions.

Go: Great morning routines include some type of exercise, whether it's a short walk, some energy-generating jumping jacks with your kids, or a full-on exercise routine. There are so many resources today, it's extremely easy to include exercise in your life. Even following a five- to ten-minute exercise video on YouTube on your phone is great.

The order and magnitude of the Seven Gs are up to you. You can certainly be flexible in how you incorporate each practice for yourself and your children. I will lay out a sample schedule that a family with eight children has shared with me.

Sample Morning Routine for a Large Family

6:00 a.m. – Mom and Dad wake up, exercise, shower, get dressed and begin making breakfast until 7:00 a.m.

6:30 a.m. – Mom and Dad wake up the school kids. School kids shower and/or get dressed and older ones help prepare breakfast. (Clothes are ready from night before – see Command Center chapter.) Older kids are helping younger kids get ready.

7:00 a.m. – Family all comes together for family meditation and affirmations

7:10 a.m. – Family talks about (and plans their day) also everyone takes turns expressing what they appreciate about a certain theme. Planned quotes or scriptures are read and briefly discussed.

7:20 a.m. – Family prayer

7:25 a.m. – Everyone eats breakfast (kids are all dressed and ready to go). Breakfast might be scrambled eggs, salad or vegetable, toast, and a fruit. Again, many options here.

7:35 a.m. – Kids perform After-Meal Cleanup and have the kitchen clean in less than ten minutes (see After-Meal Cleanup process later in the book).

7:45 a.m. – Family leaves the house. Kids get dropped off at school that starts at 8:10 a.m. Mom and Dad go to work or come back home to start the rest of their day.

The specifics of this schedule are flexible and, depending on your life schedule, can be adjusted as needed. Notice how fast things can happen. I have helped different families tailor their schedule to fit their needs and lifestyle. Many schools start at different times and the schedule can be adjusted, of course. If the mornings are tight, you can include some of the things (such as reading) in the afternoon or evening routine instead. However, if you want to have an *amazing* morning, include all Seven

Gs in your family's mornings. It will take planning and being deliberate.

The After-Meal Process

I don't know how many people have experienced this on a Saturday morning. It's almost noon. The kitchen is a disaster. The house is a mess. Mom has told the kids several times to clean up the dishes (which include the ones from the night before) and take care of their clothes. There are no kids in sight other than through the kitchen window where you can see about three of them jumping on the trampoline in the backyard. Mom's been nagging the kids all morning. The kids have basically ignored her (which is not good). And when one of them finally does walk into the room, they take the full wrath of the frustration. This was our house the Saturday I designed the After-Meal Process.

To make any process work, you must understand the three big steps introduced earlier in the book. They are:

1. Vision. Understanding what *exactly* you are after. Often, it's hard to think of or clarify specifically enough what you are after and that's OK, *as long as* you start with abstract vision (or vision-results) and drill down into the specifics enough to take clear action. Too many visions are just abstract. Many seem specific, but ask yourself the question,

"If I had a video camera and was recording the final results, what would I see?" "What does it look like?" "How is it done?" "To what level or standard is it done?" "How long does it take?" "What's realistic in the performance and execution?" "What has to happen?" and so on. Typically, people spend far less time on vision than is adequate. Spend some time to *really* understand and see what the final outcomes and results are.

2. Process. What processes are needed to create that vision? It has nothing to do with people or positions yet. This is the "how" something is achieved. If you don't exactly know how yet, get as deep as you can. At least you have a clear vision or target to go for. One thing that is helpful is to break it up in *Areas of Management*, or logical groups of procedures, tasks, or processes. I will show an example of this in our After-Meal Process. For now, just understand the concept and importance of identifying the steps, procedures, or tasks that can be grouped in an area of management, to accomplish the vision.

3. People. Now is the time to identify the skills, knowledge, and abilities that are required to *execute* those processes. You might need some expertise that you don't have or don't know. But, you know

the vision and you have at least identified the processes to get there the best you can. Often, you will need the help of an expert to help you bring it to a point where you can run it yourself. What I'm about to tell you is critical in creating your team to execute at incredible levels and where they will perform above and beyond your expectations, especially your children. And that is this: *clearly communicate the entire vision to your entire team.*

Most of the time, parents do two different versions of the same thing. They either make a list of tasks/chores/jobs and assign a kid to each one and tell them to go do it. Or, they make a list of kids and assign tasks/chores/jobs to the kids and tell them to go do it. This does not necessarily encourage teamwork. Each child is only looking out for their own – only concerned for themselves, and how they can do what *they* want to do. This might look like them trying to hurry with their chores so they can go out and play, which is great, other than they are not working together or even concerned with how the others are doing. In fact, they might even be hindering others meeting their own goals. Or worse, the child just goes out and plays without doing his responsibility at all and then you have multiple issues being conditioned in your children.

When I first did the After-Meal Process on that frustrating Saturday morning, five kids (ages six to fifteen) were able to finish the *entire* kitchen in just 9 minutes and 29 seconds. This was the *first* time these kids did the process, ever. I just invented it that morning.

Now, at first, this might seem impossible. And, in fact, we didn't think it was possible to start with, either. It also might seem unbelievable except that I've trained dozens of other families and they have repeated the result (their own completely clean kitchen in under ten minutes) after only *one* training session. I also need to point out that it took me an hour and a half to *train* the kids before they started cleaning anything. It will also, likely, take you a long time to train your kids the first time. And then you have ten-minute cleaning sessions that are productive, fun, and effective for the rest of your life.

Steps of the After-Meal Process

Vision

1. One of the first things I did was explain to the kids their responsibility, as members of our family and members of this household, to contribute, and how each family member, including the parents, have contribution obligations. This can take as long as is needed for them to clearly understand their obligation.

2. I spent *a lot* of time talking about the vision of the kitchen. I explained it to *all* the kids. I carefully went through the kitchen and we made decisions together about the vision of the kitchen. For example, I asked, "Should the chairs be tucked under that table when it's done, or should we have them upside down on top of the table?" With the input of everyone, we decided that tucked under the table looked better and was safer (one of the kids mentioned that a small kid could pull a chair on top of them if it was on the table). I pointed out the big mess in the kitchen and asked, "What is the vision of the kitchen? How should it look when we are done?" "Should the cupboards be opened or closed?" Now, of course they should be closed, but it is *critical* that the kids can see in their *own* mind what the vision is. Ask questions and guide the kids to answer them in a way that makes sense. Even ask obvious questions where they can go through the vision thinking in their own minds. Their own suggestions also help them own the vision and learn how to *think* about what it should be. You will be amazed at what they can come up with. Again, most people don't spend enough time on the vision of anything. They typically jump in and start and wonder why they miss the mark that they haven't even identified. Or worse, they never

start at all. That first training I had with my kids, I spent about 45 minutes of the total 90 of teaching on just the vision. We talked about *everything*. The stove, the fridge, the floor, where the toaster should go, what the blender should look like, how clean the stove top should be, how it should smell, what is on or in the sink, sanitation, everything. What principles are we living while we are doing the process and when it's completed? What does it look like to live those principles? (responsibility, charity, encouragement, compassion, etc.) We describe what it looks like to have compassion. How do we talk? What do we do if we see that someone needs help with their process during and after we've completed our process? Are we hindering or helping the ones around us? What if we're standing and completing the dishes and someone needs to sweep where we're standing, what do we do? What if someone is taking out trash and we need to put garbage in the garbage can and there's no bag, what do we do? What words do we speak, and how are they spoken? What is our performance level? How fast are we moving? How fast are our hands moving when we are washing countertops? How do we wash the countertop and what does it feel like when we are done? Do we stack chairs on the table to sweep? If so, why?

How do we hold the broom when sweeping? How fast is the broom moving? How detailed do we sweep? What do the corners look like? What do the corners of the counter look like? What level are we cleaning to? What soaps and cleaners do we use and why? Are we just getting things wet or are we disinfecting and getting rid of bacteria? How do we load the dishwasher? Do we rinse the dishes beforehand? If so, when and why? Where do we place the dishes inside the dishwasher and why? Why do we stack and place the dishes as we do in the cupboards and doors? How does it make the kitchen run more efficiently in preparing a meal? What tools do we use to scrub pans? *Everything*.

Process

Identify the processes that are needed to accomplish the vision. To help you out, I will just tell you the seven processes we came up with to answer this question. But, these are not set in stone. In fact, most households have slightly different ones than these. How do I know something should be a process? Simple, a process is a grouping of similar tasks. You can mix or match these or come up with your own. The seven kitchen processes we have are:

- Floor: This included sweeping, mopping, and taking care of anything on the floor.
- Put Away Good Things: This included taking care of leftovers or anything else that needed to be put away. Backpacks, books, shoes, anything of value that had to be put in its place that wasn't a kitchen item was included.
- Surfaces: Clean and sanitize all top surfaces including table, counter, stove, high-chairs, table chairs, etc.
- Large Dish Items: Take care of and wash large or odd-shaped dish items, such as blenders, cookie sheets, pans, food processors, cutting boards, etc.
- Dishes: Washing and putting away all the dishes, including loading the dishwasher and/or washing them in the sink.
- Appliances (Large and Small): Washing the refrigerator door, washing the toaster, blender base, dishwasher door, and any other appliances. Also, making sure they are put where they are supposed to be (based on our vision).
- Garbage: Basically, just taking out the garbage (usually multiple times) and ending up with a clean, fresh garbage can with a sack.

Go through the steps and expectations of each process and make sure they match the vision. Then make sure you have the supplies and equipment you need to run each process. How many dish rags do you need? Where is the broom and mop? How will you sanitize? Make sure you have all the cleaning supplies ready to run the processes before you start.

People

1. Next, you assign which kid will *start* which process – not, which kid will *do* which process. This is a critical distinction. Remember, all the kids know the vision. And all the kids are responsible to create that vision. So, when you assign which process they will *start*, it means that they will also support and *do* the other processes as needed. There was a large family I worked with that hadn't cleaned the kitchen for a week and they had a large kitchen and a lot of dishes. I went through about an hour and twenty minutes of training the vision and identified the processes, just like I had done with other families. They came up with very similar, but slightly different processes than our original seven and we were ready to start. With the idea of owning the vision instead of owning a chore, the kids set up *three* dish washing stations on the counter because everything else was getting done and the dirty dishes were the bottleneck. They were able to complete the entire kitchen in 58

minutes and 59 seconds. Because they owned the vision, all the kids were able to contribute and still get to the vision fast with just one sink. Often, when people are focused on the real, clear, defined vision, they can be quite creatively to get there with any perceived limitations they might have.

2. Before you begin, start with high energy. Have the kids all stand up and smile and look up for ten seconds. Next, have them do 10 jumping jacks, and be exciting and thrilling as you do this step. You may even put on some very upbeat music.

3. Time them. Pull out your phone and have the kids line up like they are about to jump out of the starting block. "On your mark. Get set. Go!" and start the timer.

4. Encourage them all along the way so they are excited to accomplish the vision you so effectively burned in their minds. Encourage them to keep up the energy and move fast. Call out the time every 30 or 40 seconds, encouraging them to keep going. If they go longer than ten minutes (or whatever your goal is), keep encouraging them that it's OK and to keep going.

5. *Everyone* keeps working until the entire vision is accomplished (remember the three washing stations) and have *everyone* come together at the end before you stop time.

6. At the end, congratulate them and ask, "What went well?" Discuss all the great things they did, how amazing it felt, what they accomplished, etc.

7. After that, ask, "What can we improve on?" Discuss improvements in preparation. Maybe they needed more soap or rags. Discuss improvements on process. Maybe they need to wash the counter by the sink before anything else to stack more dishes. Each kitchen is different, and this process allows for the flexibility you need.

That is the basic After-Meal Process. One of the magical things I saw when I first did this with my children was I witnessed them working together and supporting each other in what they were trying to accomplish. For example, the one doing the floor missed a spot under the table and the one doing the surfaces jumped under the table and took care of it without anyone asking them to. The one doing the floor was mindful of the one doing the dishes to allow them to open and close the dishwasher door as they needed. All this happened without me telling them to. They knew the vision and they owned it and they worked harmoniously together to accomplish it. It is a beautiful thing to see.

We also decided that because we can do the After-Meal Process so fast, we would commit to do it after *every* meal. This is how a family is able to clean up the kitchen after breakfast in under ten minutes in their morning routine. You can also use this same idea to clean or take care of any part of the house.

Bedtime Routine

I had a friend that was having trouble with his three-year-old son Michael in taking naps or, sometimes, going to bed. I want to share his story along with the solutions to help them.

Currently:

Little Michael takes naps at 2:30 p.m. for about an hour or an hour and a half in his crib upstairs in his room. He often protests, fusses, and cries just before going to nap. Mom usually puts him to nap and Dad puts him to bed about 95% of the time.

His schedule is: Up at around 7:00-7:30 a.m., breakfast at 8:00 a.m., lunch at 12:00 p.m., nap at 2:30 p.m., dinner at 6:00 p.m. and bed between 8:00-8:30 p.m. He is currently not on a bottle or binky and has "special buddies" that he likes in his crib with him.

In his nap routine, Mom or Dad tells Michael, "In a few minutes, you have to go up to your nap so we can play for 5 more minutes and then we are going upstairs." Then when it's time to go upstairs, they say, "OK, it's time to go upstairs," and this is where he is often resistant and crying. He sometimes settles down when he gets upstairs and just goes to sleep when he is put under the covers. He communicates when he fusses and protests and sometimes reverts to communicating like a cat. He'll be super quiet and then say, "Meow." Then he is told to "use his words." He usually has a problem with naps whether Mom or Dad puts him to nap, especially at the beginning.

Michael does much better in the bedtime routine and most of the time goes to bed and sleeps fine. Parents tell him, "We are going to clean up in five minutes," then they have him help clean up and go to the bath first (Dad helps him). Then PJs and brush teeth and Dad sings to him while he lays his head on his shoulders. Dad then tucks him in and he goes to sleep. Michael sometimes protests going to sleep, but is fine when he gets in the bath. Michael will sometimes cry if Dad didn't "tuck" him in all the way and he'll escalate and then calm down if Dad closes the door anyway. This only happens about 5% of time as Dad is pretty good at consistently tucking him in.

Michael's behavior is fairly consistent as described when Mom and Dad or both are there with him. However, when it is *just* Mom, Michael is usually really behaved. He is generally not as well behaved when Dad is around. Dad often lets him get away with a little more than Mom does (extra snacks before dinner, etc.).

After I understood what was going on with Michael, I suggested they carefully consider eleven points to apply to his situation as outlined next.

Suggestions for Michael:

I will list several potential issues and suggestions that may apply to varying degrees in this situation. However, rest assured that each suggestion can be specifically tailored to you and your family and I recommend you carefully consider and try each one, to the degree it makes sense, to get the results you are after. Often it is not just one thing, but a combination of several things together.

The Eight-Minute Rule:

They are already using this tool! Great! Just a reminder of the purpose and the use of it and to remember the *spirit* of the law not just the *letter* of the law. The purpose is to get the child mentally ready for a shift in activity and focus and to help him do that while being obedient to his parents. And if he knows that it's coming very soon, he will begin to transition. Of course, this is not guaranteed, and it doesn't have to be exactly eight minutes (they use 5 minutes). You can also maintain integrity by using words like "...it will be time to clean up in about eight minutes" as opposed to "...we are going to clean up in 8 minutes." On the latter, if you don't start cleaning up in *exactly* eight minutes, the validity of your words drops because you didn't do exactly as you said you would. If you say it will be *time* to clean up in *about* eight minutes, then if you don't start until ten or eleven minutes, your words still have integrity because it was only *time* to clean up at eight minutes even though you started at ten or eleven, and you still meet your purpose.

Setting the Child up to Succeed:

This is extremely critical and is not just during a certain time like naps. Most parents can improve tremendously in this area. That basic idea is simple and that is: Say what you really mean and really mean what you say. Set it up so your child can actually do what you are telling or expecting him to do. For example, I will hear a parent tell the child, "Be quiet," when they actually mean something else like, "Be more quiet," or "Be respectful," or "Talk nice," or "You need to settle down more," or something like that. It is unrealistic to actually expect a small child to be perfectly silent for very long. And then, it just becomes a struggle and neither the parent nor the child has integrity through the ordeal. This is *not* to say to "soften" all your commands. Just be ready to back up and follow through on each one. Absolutes are also important for your children. But, you need to follow through on them. It is also better to give far *less* commands that you actually follow-up on, than to give a bunch of commands. Be mindful of *all* the words you are saying to or around your children.

Giving a Command:

Everything you command your child to do, you are either training obedience or disobedience. This is closely related to setting your child up to succeed. If the child is used to being told things the parent doesn't actually mean, they are used to either being confused or being disobedient or defiant. If this is the case, they are strongly conditioned to always having a problem. This can manifest in more severe consequences as they get older. A parent needs to be *very* mindful of what he or she is saying to the children and make sure of a couple of things:

- Is it possible to accomplish given the expected parameters? (time, etc.)
- Is it possible for your child to accomplish it? (abilities, etc.)
- Does your child understand what it means? (effective communication, etc.)

Often the parent has to make up the difference for any one or more of these for the child to be in compliance. For example, if the parent says, "It's time to pick up your toys now," then sometimes the parent will take their little hand and go through the motions of picking up the toys with them, so the child can comply and be obedient to the command.

Command versus Question:

Related to giving a command, it is critical at the younger ages (1-7 years old) that the parents are aware of the type of wording they use when communicating with their child. Often parents will ask a question where they really expect a certain answer (say what you really mean). For example, if a parent asks, "Would you like to eat dinner now?" when they really mean "It's time to eat dinner," it gives the child too much freedom in decisions that they are not mature enough to make yet. If it's time to eat dinner, it's time to eat dinner. A parent might ask if they want a red plate or a green plate but should *not* ask if they want a plate when setting up for dinner.

Different for Dad:

Children are *very* smart. And they know where *each* parent's lines are and how to get there. Even if Dad only gives in rarely or if Dad changes the routine rarely, children will strive for that again if it was rewarding to them. Dad might watch the subtle actions that Mom takes (as long as little Michael can't see or hear you) that make the difference for when he does well. Also, Michael already has strong anchors to Dad and how he does things. So, Dad will need to be *very* consistent in order to change Michael's expectations with Dad. It might even get a little worse to start with if he escalates to try to get Dad to budge. As long as Dad stays with it, it *will* get better.

Discipline:

Discipline is simply communicating with your child that things need to be different in a convincing way that changes their state. With older children especially, this can be a talking to or loss of privileges. With younger children, they need to understand when something is wrong or not good. This can happen in a large number of ways. Tone of voice is *very* important and powerful. A firm, deep voice can communicate that expectations are not being met and things need to be different. Sometimes a swat or squeeze on the hand is necessary. Sometimes, quickly standing them up as you speak is a way to change their state and get them receptive. By the time they are three years old, you likely already have many discipline techniques that you are currently using.

Diet:

There are so many experts in this area. As you know, if your child has any type of sugar, it *dramatically* reduces the effectiveness of trying to get him to comply about taking a nap. Just be very mindful of what he has eaten in the day and take steps to have good nutrition as a high priority in your family.

Talking with Respect:

It is *very* important that children learn how to speak and treat their parents with respect. If a child has little respect for one or both parents, he can often step outside of his freedoms and do things inappropriately just because *he* wants to. Children have limited capacity to judge, and they must have the tie to their parents to guide them. A lack of respect fosters a lack of trust. A child that respects their parent(s), trusts their parent(s). Thankfully, children are prone to trust their parents. Often, respect has to be taught. Never let your child talk in a disrespectful tone, use disrespectful words, or jest inappropriately with the parents. It also needs to be a united front. Mom needs to make sure he respects Dad and Dad needs to respect Mom. It's also important that he sees that Dad respects Mom and expects him to, also, and that Mom respects Dad and she expects him to respect Dad. When a child escalates, watch that he practices this as much as possible; however, most of this training needs to happen when there is *not* an issue, and everyone is just living everyday life.

Routine:

Of course, the routine needs to be very consistent. You may already be doing a pretty good job at this, except when you're not. Sleep itself is a biological routine. If you can transition to a consistent routine for a period of time *before* nap time, it will come naturally most of time. Pay careful attention to the *specifics* of the routine. Do it several times, as you will see new things every time you pay attention to it. And *stick with it*! Of course, if/when you see that adjustments are needed, go ahead and make them, then *stick with it* again.

More or Less Energy:

You have to carefully judge and decide if the child needs *more* energy or *less* energy when he escalates. Each child is different. Some will just suck up the energy and take the discipline and it doesn't seem to help in the behavior or the training. If this is the case, this child needs *less* energy. This often looks like the parent silently helping the child go to bed with no eye contact and helping them to comply with the command as stated earlier (although, it is still helpful to give positive energy *if* the child complies in the expected way on their own). Or, after you put him down for a nap, you stop talking and just close the door and leave. If he keeps crying, you just ignore it (as long as it's safe to do so, of course). At first, this might seem challenging to do, but if this child needs *less* energy to comply, it will get better each time and he will understand and comply with the expectation.

Building the Moral Warehouse:

Raising children is one of the most rewarding things we can enjoy! Building the moral warehouse is stocking the mental shelves of our children with principles and ideas throughout the entire day that help them to have the right perspective on things.

You might talk to your child during the day (*not* just at nap time) about nap time and how awesome naps are, how much he loves them, how he can go to dreamland, how comfy it is, how cool his "special friends" are, etc. And condition him to look forward to naps long before he actually "gets" to take a nap. This alone can be very powerful.

Of course, life happens, and things come up every day. One day it might be more of an issue in one area and the next day it's a different thing. Be patient and consistent and you will get better overall results. Carefully consider each of these and what makes the most sense for you and your children.

Michael's Results

Since going through the above suggestions, Michael's parents have dramatically improved Michael's sleep and nap routine. Michael has more certainty and expectation of what it will be like and is thrilled to spend this special time with Mom and Dad.

Review the eleven points to set up the bedtime routine for success in your family. Use what applies, works, and make sense to you. It's also very helpful to plan a specific evening routine schedule that your kids will get used to following. I include a sample bedtime routine here; however, it's important to make the bedtime routine your own. Put your own schedule together that works best for your family.

Sample Evening Routine

5:00 p.m. Start Command Center (See Chapter on Command Center)
Everyone at home needs to be there at starting time

7:00 p.m. Meditation, Affirmations, or Declarations
Everyone in the household needs to come. Also, we do a final check-off of Command Center

7:10-7:45 p.m. Dinner

7:45 p.m. After Meal Clean-up
Sometimes alternate boys and girls, or we all get in and do it together

8:00 p.m. Free Time
Kids have the freedom for free time (outside, games, cards, developing talents: piano, keyboard, drawing, animating, etc.) Computer time: only with permission, must be appropriate, kids who still have homework to do have first priority. Mom gets to have free time too.

9:00 p.m. Quick Clean
Clean up anything that was played with for free time

9:05 p.m. Get ready for Bed
Night clothes, verify clothes are ready for the next day (this should have happened in the Command Center), wash up, and brush teeth

9:20 p.m. Daily Reflection
Entire family comes together to discuss how the day went (what went well, what we need to improve on) and go over any plans for tomorrow.

9:30 p.m. Family Prayer and Good night hug and kiss from Mom and Dad

9:35 p.m. Personal Prayers – Go to bed
Younger kids have lights out, Older kids (high school, college) sometimes need to study, work on homework.

Teenagers usually shower during this time (younger kids bathe in morning)

9:35 p.m. Dad and Mom Daily Close-out and personal planning for tomorrow
Sometimes this ends up being one-on-one time for kids that need to talk with parents about what's going on in their life, school, spiritual, next steps, etc.

10:00 p.m. Lights out for Household

CHAPTER 5:

The Command Center

"Nothing will work unless you do."
– MAYA ANGELOU

A Powerful Process: The Command Center

The reason the Command Center has its own chapter is because it's a special routine that accomplishes many important things. The Command Center can be done in the afternoon, early evening, or even right before bed. One of the reasons the Command Center is so important is because it helps answer the questions, "How do I include everything in my child's life that they need?" Children have busy lives as it is. What if my child is, or I want to have them become, excellent in a sport, or a musical instrument? How do I get my child to excel in a particular hobby or talent?

The answer is the Command Center. The Command Center brings it to life. The Command Center puts it in a place in your children's minds and hearts where they can actually perform. It also brings some structure for you and the kids to make it possible. When the Command Center is set up, the kids love it. They love to do it and get it done fast.

I recommend allowing flexibility to have the Command Center take as long or as short as you need within reason. The recommended time length is about one to one and a half hours. Again, it can be longer or shorter depending on the need for that day which I will get into more detail later. For example, if the kids get home from school at 4:00, you might start the Command Center at 4:30 after a snack. At 6:00, the kids have included areas in their life, such as family responsibilities, ownership responsibilities (explained below), church responsibilities or responsibilities to God, developing talents, leadership, daily value, school, and many other things that you have the flexibility to include. Their free time can be guilt-free and they can still take care of the responsibilities they have.

One reason the Command Center is so powerful is its flexibility. You can set up the Command Center to do and include anything you want. You can have an emphasis on academics. You can have an emphasis on developing talents. You can have an emphasis on training, or household training, job training, or task training. Anything from how to tie your shoes for the little kids, to how to change the oil in your car for your teenagers. The Command Center can focus on extra-curricular activities, such as their sports, their school, their music, even their career.

Setting Up the Command Center

The Command Center consists of several basic elements that I will go into more detail below, they are: *Command Center Chart, Personal Checklists, Message Center, and Calendar*. I will also talk about extra elements that add to the Command Center. They are: *Job Charts, Room Vision Templates, Task Training, and Steps of Progression*.

The Command Center Chart

The Command Center Chart – This is a large wall or binder chart that includes one month with the kids' names listed on each weekly row and areas of management listed on the columns for each day (a sample Command Center Chart is shown in Appendix A). You want to identify the areas of management that need to be included in your kids' lives. The recommended areas are: *Stewardship/Ownership (younger kids) or Career (for older kids), Family, God or Church, School, Personal, Develop Talents, Daily Value, and Leadership*.

What I mean by stewardship/ownership is the kids need to begin to realize and take ownership of things they're responsible for. Now, at a young age, that can simply be their bedroom. They can be a steward or a responsible owner of their personal bedroom and belongings. You can define their ownership responsibility as they have to take care of their room. As they are older, they might have a job at a company, so this would include their job responsibilities. Their job responsibilities might be expectations like, being to work on time, performing at a certain level, getting a certain project done, etc.

The *Family* area of management might include a family job or some other responsibility to the family. It's important that each child living in the home (no matter how old they are) have some sort of contribution to the household. This can be participating in the *After-Meal Process*, or helping a young sibling put away their clothes, or tending the baby, or cleaning the living room, or garage, or whatever makes sense in your home.

God or *Church* can be set up to include God in your child's life in whatever way makes the most sense to you. It can simply be following up on a Church assignment or responsibility. It can be reading a passage or verse of scripture. It can be scripture study. It can be reading a Bible story to a younger child. It can a time of prayer or meditation. It offers a way to include God in your children's lives in a deliberate and consistent way every day.

School is a common and important area of management for almost all children. Even the ones not going to a specific educational institution should continue their learning in some way and it can be included here. Since homework can often take a long time in the evening, you can save this category for last or just require a small part, like reviewing the day's assignments with Mom, as part of the Command Center hour and then finish their homework afterward.

Personal can be flexible to include many different things, such as brushing their teeth, making their beds, or completing their personal checklists. One idea that is *highly* recommended is to have each child prepare the clothes they are going to wear the next day. This is one of the most powerful tools to have a great morning the next day. They prepare and place, in a nice, folded stack, all the clothes they plan on wearing the next day. This includes shirt, pants, underwear, sock, belt, and even shoes if they are not currently wearing them. For the younger kids, the stacks of clothes are lined up near the Command Center area or near the fireplace where Mom can see them and make sure they are going to have the right clothes to wear. The older kids can keep their stack in their room for privacy.

One of the most exciting categories is *Develop Talents*. We like to have our kids develop a musical instrument talent when they are able or interested. But, even for the small kids, we have them draw a picture, color, or paint for their Develop Talents section of the Command Center. It doesn't have to be very much time during the Command

Center hour and if they want or need more time, they can continue afterward.

The *Daily Value* category gives you a chance to focus on a character trait every day with your children. For example, in a family meeting, we talk about compassion and charity. Our daily value for the next week or two is compassion and charity. The daily value might be a quick thirty-second review of what it means to have compassion and charity with their family or it might be a short discussion with Mom or Dad, or a quick essay where they actually write about compassion. It can be anything.

Leadership is a category that can include all kinds of different things for your children based on their experience and age. It can be answering questions like: "What did I do extra today for someone else?" or "What did I improve on today?" Leadership can be self-improvement, progress on a certain goal, or a specific project.

You can add or modify any of the categories you would like that makes sense for your age of children. If you have two toddlers, and their Command Center consists of stewardship, family, God, daily value, and developing talents, their family category is helping Mom wipe the table. Their stewardship is picking up their toys in their room. God category is reading a passage in the scriptures with Mom. Personal is brushing their teeth. Daily value is talking to Mom about compassion and Mom tells them the definition of compassion. In developing talents, they're going to draw a picture and give it to Dad, and that's it. That's the Command Center for a younger age child.

The Command Center for an older kid would be much more involved in all of those areas. Their family might be cleaning the garage. Their stewardship/career might be telling their mom how many stops they had on their paper route that morning and figuring out how much money they earned that day. God and church might be reading a chapter in the Scriptures or maybe they're doing a service project for their church. Personal might be updating their journal. Maybe their daily value is talking about compassion with all their siblings. Maybe their daily value is to read and find three scripture references talking about compassion. If they have leadership, maybe they're keeping a journal of, "What are some things that I did for someone else today?" Or, "In what ways did I grow today?" Or, "What do I appreciate? Where did I notice the gifts that I received in my life and how I appreciate them?" In develop talents, they're learning to play the guitar. How many guitar lessons? Or maybe they spent 15-20 minutes on guitar lesson number three or something. Then, of course, there's school. They're getting their homework done and all other school responsibilities done. Now, again, for older kids, all of these activities might take longer than an hour. You allow the flexibility with the family of different ages and different requirements. The younger kids can finish everything and have free time while the older kids finish homework or a project they are working on.

Personal Checklists

On the Command Center Chart, there is not much more than a checkmark between the kids' names and the area of management for each day. The Personal Checklists are used to outline the actual details each child is responsible for. The Personal Checklists can be tailored and modified to include daily, weekly, and monthly tasks. I have included sample checklists in Appendix B.

Message Center

Another part of the Command Center that's important is the message center. The purpose of the message center is to have a central place in the house where everyone can see messages, announcements, or ideas, or any type of global communication you have for the household. Often this can be the refrigerator. People can use magnets to pin things onto their refrigerator. I recommend some type of whiteboard where you can write messages and notes to the kids and the kids write notes to Mom or Dad. This needs to be a central area that everyone sees, preferably near the Command Center Chart.

Calendar

A critical element of the Command Center is the family calendar. Ideally, this is near the message center (or a part of the message center) and Command Center Chart. This is where the family keeps track of schedules, events, and plans. It's helpful and creates a sense of inclusion for the family to see what events are happening even if they are personally not involved in the activity. This should be a large calendar of at least the current month with markers or pens nearby.

Job Charts

Job Charts are 3x5-inch cards that have an overview of the tasks required to complete a certain job or chore. They might also have an actual picture of what it looks like to reach the vision of the particular room or job it's for. If a child has the responsibility of completing the dining room as their family job on the Command Center, they use a job chart and have a picture of what a clean and orderly dining room looks like with the specific steps to get there. It can also have a supply list of things needed to complete the job. Job charts can be stored in a hanging pocket organizer or something else that the kids can have easy access to.

Room Vision Templates

Earlier we talked about what it means to create a vision and how powerful they are. Room Vision Templates are used to help you create a vision for each room that you can keep permanent and communicate with your children. You can include a vision description in many areas for a room such as: Safety, Order, Sanitation, Smell, Atmosphere, or even something like Feng Shui.

Task Training

Task training is an extra part that can be added to the Command Center where you can track the training of each of your children in a determined list of tasks. This list can include anything like: tying your shoes, cleaning a tub or toilet at an excellent level, organizing the garage, changing the oil in the car, mowing the lawn, anything. Often, the critical element that is missing is not the desire, but the training in performing well. This portion can be used to save time and energy while getting to a high level of performance.

Steps of Progression

What if you made a list of *everything* you wanted your child to know, learn, or experience? What would be on that list? What do you (or they) want to include in their life? What needs to be included in their life? Maybe you want your child to know how to swim by seven years of age. Maybe you want them to know your family ancestry history. Maybe you want them to develop a certain musical talent. Maybe you want them to know certain wilderness survival techniques. Steps of Progression is a life-long system of deliberately including things you want your family to focus on in their experience as they grow up. It also includes the measuring and tracking of their progression in these areas. Set up a system to measure and track (by age) what you want you kids to know, include, and experience in their life.

The Command Center in Action

The most important parts of the Command Center are the Command Center Chart, the personal checklist, the calendar, and message center. Next, I want to talk about how you execute the Command Center routine and what it actually looks like. Again, you have the Command Center Chart on the wall with the kids' names on the left in the rows and the areas of management along the top in the columns per day.

I want to talk about a couple of principles that make it work. The Command Center is a special routine in the afternoon and you need to work it out for everyone to come together all at the same time. You can't just have one kid start at 4:30 and the other kids start coming around at 4:45 or 5:00 and so on. You must come together all at once. Another thing that's important is that Mom or Dad must come and start it with them. As you get practice, and you do it for a while, you can occasionally have the kids start themselves or you can delegate one of the older kids to be in charge of the Command Center, but this needs to be rare and only after it's been going for a while with you.

One of the most rewarding times, as a parent, is to be able to spend time with our kids doing the Command Center. We can take care of the things that are important in life in a very short time with the Command Center. An hour a day is not very long to do that. Now some people might say, "Well I'm not even home at 4:30. My kids and I get home at different times. I don't get off work until 5:30 or 6:00." And all this is OK. You don't have to do it at 4:30. You can do it at any time that makes sense for you. You can also shorten the Command Center. You don't have to have every day look exactly the same. For example, a family job for one day might be they're going to clean the entire living room and another day they are going to just clean one area of the living room.

I recommend the family portion of the Command Center not take more than 20 minutes, but that's a fast 20 minutes where they're working hard. You can do the Command Center at a time when *most* of the kids are home or you can break up the times of different sections to include different ages of kids when they do get home. That might mean instead of cleaning the entire garage, maybe they're only going to clean off one or two shelves in the garage and that's OK. Be clear on what shelves those are, clean those off, and check it off when you're done, and then have a plan for tomorrow. Then tomorrow, clean off the next shelves and the next day sweep the garage, and so on. There's a whole process in getting to the vision that you don't have to do it all in the first day.

This is what it looks like. We all come together before we start. We start with high energy just like the after-meal process. You can do jumping jacks, you can sing, you can start music, or anything to start with high energy. You also keep track of the time, so you can know where everyone's at and what's going on.

One of the important parts is that Mom or Dad stays near the Command Center Chart and tells the kids, "Come back and tell me when you are done." This does a couple of things; one, it helps Mom keep track, with the kids' help, how far they are and when they're getting things done. It also helps to create a strong communication between the kids and Mom in their reporting, "OK, I'm done with my family part. I'm done with my stewardship part. I'm done with my church part. I'm done with my personal and my school," and so on. The kids can have practice of reporting to Mom, letting her know how it's going and having that be a strong habit. It also creates an opportunity for flexibility, so, for example, if something needs to change or be emphasized that particular day, Mom can make those changes while the Command Center is happening.

For example, if one of the kids is doing a family part to the job and they come back and tell Mom 20 minutes later or 25 minutes later, "OK Mom, I'm done with my family job," she might need to have a reduced time on the stewardship job, so she might say, "OK, today for your stewardship, I want you to just put away your clothes. You don't have to clean up your whole room, just put away your clothes today because we've got to go shopping for school."

So, to continue, you start with high energy, you say, "On your mark, get set, go," and then you begin. Whatever makes the most sense – you can have all the kids start their family part together, or you can have some of the kids start the family part and some of them start their stewardship, and some of them start their church – but as they do each thing, they come back and tell you when it's done. It's also going to be likely that each kid is going to finish at different times and that's why Mom needs to stick around the Command Center and be involved. The kids can also see that she is engaged in the process if Mom is by the Command Center checking off the chart as each of the kids comes and tells her each part is done. She also needs to help guide and direct what they're working on and then she needs to verify that the vision and set standard of excellence is reached. Then after all those things are done, everything's checked off for the Command Center, the kids can have guilt-free, free time. They can play outside, read a book, or watch TV, or whatever else you want to allow in the free time for your children.

Incentive Program – Proof That It Matters

The goal and purpose of an incentive program is to prove to your family that what they do matters. When they see an immediate reward (the _type_ of reward doesn't make that much difference as long as it's meaningful and appropriate), they can see that it matters when they do the Command Center quickly and at an excellent level.

Having an incentive program could be the difference that makes a successful Command Center. Everyone (especially younger kids with a limited understanding) need to see a positive result when they do something right. We all need to see that what we do matters and makes a difference.

Even loving words of appreciation can be your incentive program. Every so often, have the kids do the Command Center without any reward. Help them appreciate how good it feels to have a clean house and have all their responsibilities done. The real reward is in doing the right thing. Remind them often the reason we do the Command Center.

You can have individual incentives, or incentives for the whole family, or both. Maybe your incentive will be a trip to the park, or a family game night if the whole family completes their Command Center on time for a week. For younger children, you need to have an incentive program that allows them to get the results daily. Have a simple prize (like a small piece of candy or crackers) for the ones that are too young to understand the concept of saving up and buying a prize with tickets. Some important ideas to remember with the incentive program you choose: 1) If you reward them for each item they do on their checklist, they will only pick the ones they want to do, and other important items will not get done. Rather, you could reward for "the whole morning being done," etc. 2) Don't create an incentive program that is going to be impossible for you to maintain, or unlikely for the kids to reach. 3) If you wait to reward until the end of the month, you will lose most of them. It is too far away. (Even the end of the week is too far away for little kids; they need a chance to earn something daily.) 4) Too much reward creates entitlement. Always keep the fundamental principles and reasons at the forefront of why they are doing what they are doing.

CHAPTER 6:

Setting Up Your Home Environment

"Be a yardstick of quality. Some people aren't used to an environment where excellence is expected."

– STEVE JOBS

Home Environment

Home environment is so important. The environment your kids exist in creates their world and their perspective on the rest of their life. You must set up the environment to succeed. Someone that is trying to lose weight will have the most success if their environment is set up to support their efforts. If they have a box of donuts on the kitchen table, it's not going to work very well. Sometimes they are going to resist and not touch those donuts. But, it's going to be extremely difficult to succeed with donuts in their environment.

The same is true in all parts of life. The things that we surround ourselves with, the things that we experience, all influence our perspective and focus no matter who we are or how good or how strong we think we are or even how disciplined we are. Our environment does affect us. And of course, this is true for our children. Our home is the most important and most powerful environment that they have.

Pictures on the Wall

There are a lot of different elements of the home environment. Consider the things that we have on our walls. Literally the pictures, or the sayings, or even the colors that we have on our walls. I knew a family once that had a teenager that painted her walls all black. Of course, she also dyed her hair black and she surrounded herself with negative things. She had some very serious challenges. It might seem strange to attribute a teenager's room paint color to their personal problems. Which came first? The black walls or the rebellious attitude? We all might be able to think of someone that would fit either case.

I was talking with a mother with a ten-year-old son that kept having nightmares. He would also be generally negative during the day. To resolve it, we did a couple of things. I recommended that she change the mattress to be more comfortable. She replaced the light in his room with a higher wattage light so it was brighter. And she also arranged his bedroom so he could have a place to put everything and his bedroom could be clean. She also added a live plant in his room that he would help take care of (it's a good idea to choose a plant that is *easy* for a ten-year-old to take care of.) Finally, I had him imagine the monsters in his dreams wearing ballerina tutus and making "boing-boing" sounds and flowers growing up out of the ground wherever they stepped. His nightmares stopped.

The home environment influences and affects pretty much every part of life. It's important that we maximize the positive effect of our home environment. One of those things on our walls is our family pictures. I remember as a kid when I was just five years old, I would see a picture of Mom and Dad holding hands walking along a stream in a forest. The picture had an inlay of them hugging and holding each other, looking down at the stream. When I looked at that picture, I saw how happy they are, and I thought, "Wow, they really love each other." That was one of the things that showed me what love looked like in my young mind. All through the years of my childhood, they had that picture up on the wall, and it meant a lot to me as a child and as I got older. It was just a picture they had of themselves, holding hands and loving each other.

Make sure you have on your walls pictures of you (Mom and Dad) – holding each other, loving each other – and things that the kids can look at and admire.

The things on the walls are the things that your children will aspire to. For example, if one of your young teenagers wants to put a picture of their favorite lead singer on the wall, you need to think about some very important questions first. "What will my child aspire to having that person's picture on the wall?" or "Is that person someone I want my family or my child to aspire to?" and if answer is yes, then have the picture on the wall. But if the answer is no, then find another thing or person that your children will want to aspire to. The reason they're putting that picture on the wall in the first place is because they like that person. And we like people that are either like us or people we want to be like.

Your child might think that they like that person, but what they *actually* like are the emotions and the feelings they feel when they listen to their songs. Music is one of the most powerful influencers. It's kind of a two-edged sword. As someone listens to a song and they like it, it has an impact and an influence on their heart and on their mind, especially their unconscious mind. Now, if they recognize the singer and like or love the singer that's singing that song, and they put a picture of that singer on their wall, then the thing that you have to be conscious of is they're not just linking or aspiring to the song and the feelings it makes them feel, but they're aspiring to that actual person. It is very unlikely that the popular singers of today have all the ideals and standards you want your child or your family to have. I would recommend not putting any pictures of singers on the wall unless, of course, they are a singer that not only sings great songs, but also has a life and habits in their personal life that you want your child to aspire to.

Again, recognize what's happening. If the child likes a particular song, they like the feelings that that song makes them feel, it's not necessarily the person or the singer. You need to be careful to help your child understand this and how far their affection or admiration for the singer goes.

Instead, you can have uplifting sayings, pretty landscapes, family pictures, ancestral pictures, pictures of Jesus, pictures of nature, pictures of your extended family, family heirlooms, family awards, placards, certificates and so on. Fill your walls with images and beauty that inspire the life you'd like your children to lead.

Music

Another critically important element of environment is music. I'm not just talking about music playing in the home over the loud speaker. I'm talking about the music that your children listen to on their iPods; the music they watch and listen to on YouTube; and the music that they include in their life. There are a number of studies that show that music is one of the most, if not *the* most, powerful communicators to the unconscious mind, both positive and negative. There are meditation teachers that use music to get people into a meditative state. Almost all music affects our brainwaves. Music affects our moods. With music, our minds are more susceptible to the influence of the words and experiences with it. Music is an extremely important element to take care of in the environment of your children.

Now where does that primarily come from? It comes from three main places: first, from you as their parents. What do you allow in your house? What music do you listen to in the car? What music do you like and why do you like it? As parents, we need to be wise in our music choices and their influence. There's a lot of music where the music isn't that good, but we're used to it, we like it, and if we think about the lyrics, they aren't very good, or it's not the type of music we want to have influencing our children.

The second place that it comes from are their friends. Obviously mostly from school, but it also might be their family friends, their cousins, or their babysitters, or places that they go that they can hear or be influenced by music. We need to help our children develop the tools they need to judge what music is good and what isn't and why. Help them understand why it's good. Help them to see and make conscious decisions of how they're going to be as they go through an experience with music or they understand certain lyrics.

The third place is the rest of their environment. What experiences are they participating in on their leisure time (movies, outings, etc.)? We have to make a decision of what we want to include in our children's lives. We also have to be conscious and countermeasure influences that take them in a direction you don't want to go.

I recommend having some uplifting music, some calming music, some music that brings, you might say, the right spirit in the house, brings the right emotions, and brings the right direction of where you want your family to go. I also recommend that children are required to share with their parents the music they download or have stored on their mobile devices.

Internet and Media

Some of the most powerful influences of our children's environment in modern society are the Internet, social media, and electronic devices. I've seen two-year-olds handle a touchscreen phone and play videogame apps or start music and it's just a normal, everyday thing. Even twenty years ago, this simply did not exist.

We have to be extremely conscious of the Internet exposure and the things going on with our children online. I recommend several ideas to manage this effectively. One, there are no computers in any bedrooms. The reason is so there are no private computers except in Mom and Dad's room. Computers are public and visible by Mom and Dad, and everything happening on the Internet is something that can be in public. If there are some private emails or correspondence that need to happen, it can be done on the parent's computer or on their personal device for the older kids that have a mobile device contract. You will eliminate a great deal of the risk and still be able to use the Internet as needed.

What about their phones? I recommend having a mobile phone or mobile device contract. I got this idea from a family that does an excellent job of managing their media and Internet exposure, and what they do is have their teenagers agree to and sign a mobile device contract. Their younger children don't get personal phones. Some conditions of the contract are, first, they actually need it. Second, they agree to uphold the family standards and ideals in the use of the phone in a way that honors the family. This includes accessing appropriate websites and using it for positive or productive things. Third, the parents have full access and passwords to the device and all their social media and app accounts.

The teenagers also have the same type of contract for each social media account they have. They have to have a clear and compelling reason to have it. They uphold the family ideals. And they give the parents full access to the accounts. Parents need to have an outstanding relationship with their teenager for this to work. Teens that feel like they are not trusted or are constantly being ridiculed by their parents are not going to comply with this recommendation very well. Parents need to be wise and careful with the hearts of their children and help their character develop before their experience and when they do experience, parents help them get to the next step in a productive way. Another family turns off their Wi-Fi after 10:00 pm to help manage Internet usage.

I recommend that parents periodically review all the accounts of their children. If there are any issues, now is the time to bring the character up above the experience. So if there are any issues, talk to the kids about Internet dangers. Talk to the kids about their virtue and the appropriateness of what they are exposed to on the Internet and how to protect themselves so that they can be equipped to make the right decisions.

Nurturing

Another important part of the home environment is actual nurturing, including physical nurturing of your children. I think everyone has heard of the problem of failure to thrive syndrome in infants. Basically, if a baby is born and is never touched, held, or hugged, then they die, even with adequate food. They will eventually die from failure to thrive, and there's not really a complete explanation of why that is, but it's true.

This is also true as our children grow up. It's important to have a nurturing and loving environment. Of course, that means a comfortable bed, warm blankets, adequate clothes and shoes, and basic necessities of life. It's also important to have appropriate, loving physical contact. Part of physical nurturing is hugging your kids. Give them a hug often. Each kid is different on the length of hug they need. Some just need a quick squeeze and some need several seconds to minutes.

It's easy to tell. Just gently hug your child and don't stop until they start to let go and you notice that they are good. Give them what they need in this area and it will make a huge difference. Give them a hug good night and good morning. You can tuck them into bed. Give them a hug when you leave, or give them a kiss on the cheek, or a kiss on the forehead often, or have them sit close to you. Whatever chances they get, have them sit close to you, put your arm around their shoulders, and give them a squeeze. Their need for physical nurturing will change as they get older also and this is normal. Physical nurturing is critically important for the development of your child, and to have them know that they're loved. It's also important that it comes from both Mom and Dad.

Friends

Another powerful aspect in children's environment is their friends. When I think about the influence of friends as the children go through school, they often have a real need to fit in, to be a part of, and to belong to something or someone. The kids develop friendships with other people that they care about. And their friends develop relationships with them. The influence of peers is extremely powerful. And, in fact, there are times where it's likely the most powerful influencer in their life.

So how do we manage that influence as parents? I recommend beginning at a young age as the kids are starting to associate and socialize, including social media friends. Ask your child this one question as you or they decide what friends they have, or keep, or the depth of friendship, or what they include in that friendship, and so on. That question is, *"At what level does your friend choose the right thing in* _____*?"* For example, at what level do your friends choose the right thing in language? As a family, you have a certain standard of language that is expected. What words are appropriate or accepted? What words are not acceptable to say? What does it mean, and why do we say that? And at what level do we do it?

Sometimes we have to be careful. Some kids will use bad language when they're away from home, then good language when they get home. Your children need to have their character over the experience and decide what *they* are and *who* they are in their personal standards.

You can say the same question for health. At what level do your friends choose the right thing in what they eat? Do we as family drink soda pop? Do their friends drink soda pop? Well I'll tell you right now, if their friends drink soda pop, and your family doesn't, there's an extremely likely chance they are going to drink soda pop. Your child is going to be influenced to drink soda pop at least occasionally. Now you can see where this is going. At what level do your friends choose the right thing in cigarettes or drugs? If my child's friends all smoked, there is an extremely likely chance that my child will at least try smoking. If I don't want that to be included in my child's life at all, then I'm going to influence, as a parent, to not have any friends that smoke.

This is true for every part of life: the level of virtue that their friends practice, the level of compassion that their friends practice, the level of responsibility that their friends practice. Are their friends the ones that get all their homework done? Are they the kids that sluff class? Are their friends the kids that get A's and work hard? Are their friends the kids that get C's and don't care that much? We can influence, decide, and help our children decide, what type of friends they want to look for even before they encounter a social situation.

As the children get ready to go to school, you can have a discussion about friends. "They're going to be a lot of different kids in your class. There're going to be a lot of different ideals that they have. I want you to notice the type of kids, the types of things that they do, and start to notice what types of kids you want as friends. And then make a list of names of the kids in your class that will fit well in that list." You can literally preempt how your kids choose their friends and set them up to succeed and have healthy friendships. You will also use this tool to help your children reduce or eliminate the unhealthy friendships they might have.

Health

Another critically important home environment factor is health. There are a countless number of books, articles, and efforts talking about everything on health. It is beyond the scope of this book to go into the details of all the aspects related to health that affect your children. It's such a critical thing that it must be addressed and handled in your home. Do what you can to find a way to live at a high, healthy level. What does that mean? Do what it takes for you to be healthy as a parent. Our physical health affects everything in our life. Our physical health affects our mood, our emotions, our mental capacity, our physical ability. It affects everything in life. Optimize your health in a way that you can optimize everything else in your life and the lives of your children.

If your kids, for example, are having a sugary breakfast every morning, their health is being diminished. For some kids, it's worse than others, but their focus, their abilities, and their learning are affected by a sugary breakfast. Do everything you can as a parent to maximize and optimize the health of your family. There are countless ways to do it. Do the work and make a major difference in this area. Of course, consult your doctor or health care provider before making any drastic changes in your family's health practices. But make the changes that you need to make. Exercise. Do some physical activity. Drink clean water. Eliminate toxins. Eliminate things in the environment that are toxic. Some families will solve major problems in their children just by optimizing their health.

Mom and Dad Relationship

Another critical factor in the home environment is the experience that your children have as they grow up and witness the relationship of Mom and Dad. As we talked about earlier, they aspire to things on the wall, they also aspire to be like Mom and Dad at least in part. The relationship and habits of Mom and Dad affect their perspective more than almost anything else. If the relationship between Mom and Dad isn't good, then your child's world can be dramatically affected. If your child is in a home where Mom and Dad are fighting all the time, what happens to that child? One of the things that child is learning is what it means to be a husband or wife, or father, or mother. That child learns how to treat people the way Mom treats Dad and the way Dad treats Mom. They learn how to talk to people the way that Mom and Dad talk to each other. Often, we don't realize the impact that we have as parents. Our children are watching and modeling and learning everything that we do. The relationship that we have as parents with each other is critically important.

How to improve yours: One way to improve your relationship with your husband or wife is to meet their emotional needs. Often the man needs certain things to feel loved or there are certain ways that he feels loved. Some of the top ways the masculine feels loved are if he is *honored, respected, admired, appreciated,* and *loved.* And often in that order. Some of the top ways for the feminine to feel loved are if she is *loved, cherished, adored, taken care of,* and *appreciated.* This doesn't mean that they we don't like a little bit of everything. But, if these needs are met for our partners, they feel a tremendous amount of love. Give them the gift. Make it about them instead of about yourself. It will have a tremendous impact on your life and the lives of your children.

Of course, these don't necessarily have to be in this order exactly, but, for example, for most men, being respected and honored is how they feel loved or how you can communicate and show love, so if you want to show love to a man, respect, honor, or admire him. If you want to show love to a woman, love, adore, cherish, or take care of her, and she feels love. Another part to understand too is with the masculine, they tend to have a focused perspective as opposed to the feminine tendency to have a broader perspective. Feminine are able to see more at any given time, and yes, guys, girls can multitask better than you can, because they have this tendency of a broader perspective.

Often that means the feminine will put meanings in place that aren't already there. So when Dad tells Mom, "I'll be home at 7:00 on Thursday," typically what he means is exactly that, he'll be home at 7:00 on Thursday. But often what it means to the feminine, can be many things. "Well, why is he coming home at 7:00? He came home at 6:00 yesterday. Why is it 7:00 today? Why did he call me and tell me? Why didn't he text me? Why did he text me? Why didn't he call me?" And there's all kinds of meanings going on typically in a feminine's mind. Now, of course, as a mature feminine woman, she can manage those meanings and manage them in a way that is productive and effective and that can strengthen the relationship.

Also, a mature masculine can recognize there is often more going on then he might realize and be open to things his wife really needs. He is prone to try to solve, fix, or push through to the next level and *more* often she really needs you to listen, understand, and just be with her. To the man this might seem like nothing is happening or no progress is being made. The truth is, that is often how to make the most progress in reaching her heart and expressing love to her.

The other thing that's critically important in our husband-and-wife relationship is the language that we use, the words that we say, and how we say them. Language creates our meanings, which create our beliefs. The things that we say and how we say them create our world. We need to be very careful and mindful of how we talk to each other as husbands and wives, and how we talk about things to other people, and how we talk about our husband or how we talk about our wife to other people, even if we're divorced. How do we talk about people to other people? We need to identify and recognize that we have outcomes that we're after. What are our outcomes? What are our outcomes for our own relationship? What are our outcomes for what the children see and witness in our relationship? How can they be done productively in a way that is helpful to the development of our child?

For a man, one of the ways that you can connect to your wife is to be calm and connected to her. When you're literally connected with your wife in a calm way, then you're listening to her. You're with her. You're understanding and appreciating her. Often, we've heard the idea where a man wants to be the hero for his wife or his woman, and that is absolutely true. One thing to recognize, though, is that you want to be the hero of *her* story, and that requires listening and understanding. It requires listening to what her needs are and what her preferences are and what's going on in her world. Listen to what's going on in her heart and her mind, and as you do that, you can then begin to see where you can be her hero.

For a woman, one of the ways you can connect with your husband is to support, admire, and appreciate him. Often people have a tendency to expect everyone else to be perfect and when they are not perfect, people tend to miss out on the gifts that the other person is. Listen to him and support him in his efforts. Help him and support him in reaching his goals. Be vulnerable to him and allow him to help and support you. Love him unconditionally. Don't try to *change* him to progress but support him *in* his progress. Express appreciation and admiration often. Smile at him often. One of the greatest gifts you can give him is to let him know you are happy and feel loved with him or because of him. Make him your hero, whether you feel like he deserves it or not.

CHAPTER 7:

Setting up Your Family Legacy

"Your future is created by what you do today,
not tomorrow."

— ROBERT KIYOSAKI

Family Identity

In order to make things work consistently in your family, you have to create a family identity and legacy. An identity is *who* they are and what they stand for. There are several ways to do that. One thing that creates an identity is what your family, and your kids, are loyal to. Along with the principles and ideas that you talk about in your family, they also have to be consistently loyal to something. Now, of course this can include your faith, your religion, or other ideals or standards that you have. It can also include ideals that you've identified as a family.

For example, one family has, as one of their family ideals, is that they are honest. They got that from their grandfather. He said, "Honesty is not just the best policy, it's a way of life." He talked about honesty a lot, and the importance of honesty and doing a good job. The parents have kept that in their legacy ever since.

Of course, nearly all parents want their kids to be honest. But, the question is: "How much do we really talk about it, expect it, train it, and practice it so they clearly understand what it means?"

These days, clear ideals are more rare. Many families are trying to redefine themselves all the time or not really at all. They're often trying to fit in with the current culture or trying to do things in a way that fits in with the status quo of what's going on around them. This is especially true for children and adolescence. They try to find a place where they fit in. They try to find friends, and they try to belong somewhere. You can set it up so your family is the place they belong to already. If you establish a family identity, then your child can tie and link to that identity much more easily and clearly, especially through the challenges in their life.

How do you do that? There are a couple of important ways. One of those things is to meet often as a family and have family meetings. Meet and decide, train, and teach who you are and what you stand for. Teach the kids about your ancestry, teach the kids about principles. Don't just rely on the school system to do it. Don't just rely on your church to do it. And definitely don't rely on their friends or the media to do it. You teach it. You tell the kids what it means to be honest. You tell them what it means to care about somebody. You tell them what it looks like to have compassion. You tell them what it means to work hard and what's necessary to succeed in life. As you do that, there are several amazing things that can happen.

You can train and teach the example you have been, and the successes and experiences you've had. You can also train and teach your kids to avoid some of the problems that you or someone else have experienced. There are things in the past that you didn't know how to avoid at the time, and you have some amazing experience and knowledge you can share. Your kids can do better and learn from you. One of the things I recommend is to create a yearly plan of trainings and teachings that you want to include with your kids.

You might meet every week, every other week, and so on. I recommend meeting at least every two weeks. It doesn't have to be very long, it could be an hour, it could be an hour and a half, it could be a couple of hours. Have it be a meaningful and planned meeting. A special gathering where you all come together. You could open with prayer and have a specific outline and subjects you want to discuss. All the kids are expected to be there and expected to participate. If you start at a young age, they will be used to the pattern of meeting often as a family. Another thing this will do is help them feel a part of, and belong to, the family that they're in. It will help establish an identity of what your family is all about.

Family Meeting Example

One of the things that I talk about before the kids prepare to go to school is: What are the five most-important things about going to school? And they're character and principle-based. Number one is respect, obedience, and charity to their teachers. For the kids to be successful in school, especially beginning at a young age, they need to understand and respect the authority of the teacher at school. The children need to be teachable. They need to be someone that looks to someone, mainly their teacher, and is open to their teaching. And, as they do that, they begin to literally practice the principles of success for the rest of their life. They can be teachable and learn and grow and progress in whatever area of life that they have.

Number two is respect and charity for other students. Basically, acknowledge and help your child to understand the importance of treating other people well. Treating people with respect. Treating people with charity and love. Treating people with gratitude and appreciation and helping your children understand that. As they start to develop their social skills, especially at a young age, this is really important for them to have throughout the rest of their life.

Number three is respect for property. This includes honesty as well. I tell the kids that they don't go pick up a pencil that doesn't belong to them sitting on someone's desk just because it's there, even if they need it. They go and ask the person first, "May I borrow your pencil?" And they show respect for the property and ownership of the pencil. It also includes making sure that they show respect for the bathrooms and making sure that they clean up after themselves wherever they go, and that they don't damage any property. They also take care of things; they take care of their books and their desks.

My grandfather used to teach us, and say, "Don't let the kids tear up magazines, even if you're going to throw them away." The reason for that is he wanted the kids to learn how to take care of things. Technically, it would have been all right to tear up a magazine that was going in the garbage anyway, but the act of tearing the pages and ripping up the magazine conditioned and taught the kids that that's what you do with magazines whether it was going in the garbage or not. I think this is a very important part to include in the habits of your children.

Number four was to do your best. Usually, the result of doing your best will result in getting As, at least As and Bs. Oftentimes, parents will focus on just the grades, and sometimes that helps the kids, but it also sometimes misappropriates the focus of what's important. What I mean by that is sometimes kids will even be dishonest to get good grades, or they'll focus on just getting the grade instead of learning or making a difference in something that might be more important. I tell the kids to just do your best, do your very best. Do your best to get good grades, do your best to understand and learn as much as you can, do your best to please the teacher, do your best to help the kids, help your fellow students, or help the project succeed. Do your best.

Number five is do the right thing and/or stand up for what's right. When you go to school, what does that mean? This is often, of course, where most of the kids get introduced to things that test their character. We need to make sure their character is prepared for their experiences. For example, the first time they're offered a cigarette or the first time they're offered drugs. How do they handle that and answer in the most productive way? One of those things is if they choose to do the right thing. What is the right thing in that situation? What is the right thing when someone asks them to sluff class? What is the right thing when they have the opportunity to steal something? What is the right thing when someone offers them drugs? What is the right thing when they have the choice to get their homework done, to get the project done, or to go watch a movie instead? Helping them understand that one of the most important things about going to school is doing the right thing. And that's an important thing to focus on as you help your kids prepare for school.

Outings, Celebrations, and Traditions

Another thing that creates family identity is having outings, celebrations, and traditions. Set up traditions of how you celebrate holidays, for example. What do you do on Thanksgiving? What do you do for Christmas, Easter, Hanukkah, or any other holiday that you celebrate? Have those family traditions be important and be consistent.

Every summer, you could have a planned outing that was more than just a vacation. It could be themed and a time where you go over special subjects with your teenagers or do some family planning. Sometimes the outing could be a training opportunity. Sometimes the outing might be a combination where you have recreational time during the day, maybe get together and meet as a family, talk about what you appreciate, or you talk about your goals for the year, or you talk about overcoming any challenges that someone has. Doing this and sharing these experiences with your children creates a very important and critical identity in their hearts of who and what they are.

Another thing that you can do is create other types of habits or traditions. I know a father who started his family later in life, and when his children were quite young, he taught his kids square dancing. He also included music as a leisure activity. He himself played the piano, accordion, and guitar. Square dancing is not a very popular dance these days, but his family did so well that they would perform at the local schools and fairs. This did a couple of things. One is it taught the kids how to step in time, how to listen, it taught them rhythm, it got the little kids used to doing what their father told them to, and it was fun.

Recreation as a family is important. Often, we notice that how we play games is how we play life. This same square dance father taught his kids how to play card games. And they often had parties where they got the cards and board games out. They knew how to have a good time without TV or movies. If you watch the dynamic of how your children (or individual child) handles things while playing games, you will notice patterns of how they will (and do) handle life. How does each child handle someone else winning or succeeding? How does your child handle disappointment? Is your child interested in someone else doing well or are they only interested in themselves? Do they put others down, so they get ahead? Do they tend to cooperate with others? Are they compassionate? Are they mean? Are they disrespectful? Are they happy and fun to be around? Do they pout or complain? This is a *very* valuable exercise to get a glimpse of where your child's heart is in different areas. This same father also taught his kids how to work hard as well as how to play.

Sometimes my grandmother would gather up some of the grandkids and we would go help someone. She would get the grandkids on a Saturday and take them out and help someone paint some rooms in their house, or help repair a fence, or manicure the yard. She would go and just do something with her grandkids to help somebody and she emphasized that's what we are as a family. We help people. We care about what's going on. We care about the people around us. And we are the ones that do something about it.

Another thing you can do is start something that we call Make a Difference Night. It is similar to what my grandmother used to do. It's about going out and helping someone in the community. It might be a relative, it might be a neighbor, but we'd go out and make a difference. That could be a couple of things. It could be helping an elderly neighbor with a need. It could be a small home or yard improvement project. It could be delivering food to somebody. It was something where we could actually go and make a difference for somebody else to show that they mattered. We wouldn't get paid for it and we wouldn't ask to be paid for it. It would be, literally, something that we would do just to help someone else. You might schedule a Make a Difference Night every other month or maybe every quarter, or something like that. Something where the family can get together and as part of their identity, they contribute to the community, extended family, or the people around them in different ways.

Another things that's important to recognize and realize in a family legacy is that everything affects everything. It's not just the family meetings, or not just the outings. But it's everything. Talk to your kids often about who and what they are. What's expected? What possibilities do they have by living a certain way? What possibilities are limited, by living a certain way? If you want to have a certain type of child or type of family, start at a young age and describe it to them. Sometimes, as parents, we get to where we enjoy our children and we play with them and we're their friends, and we sometimes forget to be the parent and the teacher. Our children need instruction. They need example. They need to know how life is, and how to make things work. They need an identity that they can tie to. If their identity can have a foundation of your family identity, they can be more grounded, more successful, and have much more of a compelling future than they would without it.

It's also important to recognize what is needed in handling certain problems. If a problem does come up with a child, what is missing? What is the problem really? Find out and get to the root cause of the problem. Often, the root of the problem is something with their character or something with their experience they were not ready for. It might be some kind of meaning they need help and guidance in resolving. They often need help in the things they are thinking about and worrying about.

A family identity creates a family legacy. Take some time to think about what legacy you want to have and be as a family. What type of a family do you want to be known as? What type of a family do you want your kids to be? How do you want your neighbors to experience you? How do you want the kids at school to experience your children? How do you want grandma or grandpa to experience your children? Create a family legacy in a way that is compelling and gives guidance and establishes a foundation for all your efforts in raising your children.

CHAPTER 8:

When It Gets Challenging

"Before you give up, remember why you started."
– HUNTER X HUNTER

Keep Going

Doing the Command Center and consistently executing on the routines that we've talked about create a condition where it's easier to do it than not doing it. That is, it's easier to incorporate all the things you want to include in your family and get the results than it is to not get the results by not doing it. It doesn't seem like this at first because you are deliberately and slowly making the changes. As you put it together and you get used to executing it, at first, it's going to seem a little hard just because you are not used to it yet. If you stick with it, you will find that it becomes easier to do it than not doing it. However, you'll want to stop doing it sometimes, and sometimes you will. When you do, you'll find that life begins to be harder again, with more chaos and more confusion starting to creep in. When you get to that point, congratulations, because you know you are getting results in your family when you do it.

You also have the ability to be as flexible as you need, to add or subtract or modify anything that you need in your day and in your kids' experience. However, stick with the fundamentals to make things work.

I instructed a class not long ago where I asked for a list of problems that come up and why they can't do what we talked about in the book. I also asked for foreseeable obstacles that would prevent them from doing it. There were all kinds of things that came up on the list. Things like, "Well I don't get home on time," or "My kid's aren't doing very good in school, and so I have to do some extra stuff to help them do well," or, "I'm having health issues or health problems, I'm sick and I can't physically do it." Or another problem is, "I don't feel like it," or another problem is, "I don't have what I need to set it up," and so on. There were quite a variety of different problems, excuses, and reasons why they couldn't implement these ideas.

Try this out for yourself. I want you to make a list of any problems – of course you can use some of these that I've just mentioned – that you might see, either now or in the foreseeable future, that might stop you from doing and setting these things up.

Go ahead and think about *your* list. Make your own list and be sincere about it. Don't spend too much time, no more than twenty or thirty minutes at the most. Most of you can do it faster than that. Make a list of ten to twenty things that might be problems, that might prevent you from implementing these ideas. After you've done that, take a look at each item and recognize something. Recognize that almost all the things on your list are not actually problems, but symptoms. They're symptoms of the *real* problems. They're symptoms of the root cause of things that might be in your life or in your family's life that are causing some of the issues that are coming up that might be preventing you from executing.

They're symptoms of the problems that might be in your heart or mind. Root problems like not caring enough. Root problems like the relationship you have with your husband or wife. Root problems like the habits you've allowed to be in your own life. Root problems that are *actually* getting in the way and because of these root problems, you have all of these symptoms that seem like they are the cause of why you can't execute consistently. I want you to go through them and I want you to think about what is the real problem here? What causes this problem? Is there a way to prevent it? What needs to be setup? What habits or standards do I need? Is there a way to solve it? What would solve it? How would it be solved in a way that would be consistent with what you're after? If you can honestly do this exercise and think about what is a problem and what is actually a symptom, you will have an awareness of yourself that most people don't reach in their lifetime.

Work on the real problems. Maybe the real problem is not your mood as much as it is your diet. Maybe not taking care of yourself physically is what's causing problems emotionally. Maybe a problem of being tired is because you've not been able to sleep and maybe the problem of not being able to sleep is really because of the relationship that you have with your husband or wife. Get to the specific, solvable, root problem and go from there.

Energy and Joy

Life is fueled by emotion and energy. A person can fuel their life with negative energy and emotion or positive energy and emotion. As parents, one of the *greatest* gifts we will ever give our children is the ability to fuel their life with positive energy and emotion. Notice, and help them, at a young age, to have a perspective where they can see the positive and good in things. Help them to learn how to solve their problems in a productive and positive way.

Take time to celebrate and appreciate how far you've come. Notice the difference, in just the change in your mindset that has been made already. Enjoy your family and your children, keeping the principles and practices at the forefront of how you got there.

Chapter 9

Do What's Important

"The most beautiful people we have known are those who have known defeat, known suffering, known struggle, known loss, and have found their way out of the depths. These persons have an appreciation, a sensitivity, and an understanding of life that fills them with compassion, gentleness, and a deep loving concern. Beautiful people do not just happen."

– **Elisabeth Kübler Ross**

And Keep Doing It

The main thing is to remember what's important and focus on that. Face reality and start from where you are. Don't try to do it all at once. Take what's most important and focus on that first. You can focus on a few different grouped action items:

Group 1 – Setting up My Morning for Success

- Make a list of things needed to be done the night before to have a "Great" morning. This might be things like preparing exercise clothes, kids clothes are ready, sleeping environment, planned affirmations, etc.

- Plan out your morning routine. Set times to do each part in a way that makes sense for you. Implement as much as makes sense in your morning and get a great start on each day and help your kids do the same.

Group 2 – Home Environment

- Do a serious assessment of pictures and placards you have on the wall and around the house. Think about what you want the kids to aspire to and support what you are after.

- Do a health assessment of your refrigerator and cupboards and determine your family's next step in improving your health.

- Start a library of music and videos you will have available to your family.

- Organize your main living areas in your home: Living room, kitchen, family room, etc. to support the new lifestyle you are setting up for your family.

Group 3 – The Command Center

- Make a list of everything you want to include in the daily life of your family. Which of those things will be included in the Command Center routine? Which things will be in other routines (morning or bedtime)?
- Do the Command Center routine. Just start. Start simple and grow from there.

Group 4 – Begin My Family Legacy

- Make a list of topics you would like to teach and/or include in your family meetings or trainings.
- Schedule regular family meetings (at least every two weeks) on your calendar with a planned topic.
- Plan family traditions on holidays and other activities and schedule them.
- Along with the action items described, review the ideas in the book that you can use to strengthen your relationship with your spouse. Consider the needed improvements of the habits with your children of verbal tonality, physical affection, diet, bedtime habits, etc. Focus on what you know you can succeed at now and make small wins toward capturing your children's hearts. I am so excited

for your success and joy in making your family wonderful and amazing!

Further Reading

Mindset: The Psychology of Success by Carol S. Dweck

The New Dare to Discipline by Dr. James Dobson

The Talent Code: Greatness Isn't Born. It's Grown. Here's How by Daniel Coyle

The Miracle Morning: The Not-So-Obvious Secret Guaranteed to Transform Your Life (Before 8AM) by Hal Elrod

13 Things Mentally Strong Parents Don't Do: Raising Self-Assured Children and Training Their Brains for a Life of Happiness, Meaning, and Success by Amy Morin

The Happiness Advantage: How a Positive Brian Fuels Success in Work and Life by Shawn Achor

Leadership and Self-Deception: Getting out of the Box by The Arbinger Institute

Growing Kids God's Way Program by Gary and Anne Marie Ezzo

The Case Against Sugar by Gary Taubes

Acknowledgments

There are so many people to thank that have touched my life and made this book possible. My family has helped and supported me through the development of this book and the application of the concepts to make them real.

There are not enough words or written concepts that could express the gratitude I have for my parents. The people they are and the inspiration they create is hard to measure. I would also like to thank Paul for his inspiration, insights, guidance, and support in making all this possible.

The inspiration of my children to make me want to be a better father and help them have amazing lives and be amazing parents themselves is a powerful driving force. I have many mentors I want to thank. Steven Linder, Keith Cunningham, Steven Drewes, Darren Hardy, and many others have each taught me unique and invaluable lessons on my journey.

To the Morgan James Publishing team: Special thanks to David Hancock, CEO & Founder for believing in me and my message. To my Author Relations Manager, Tiffany Gibson, thanks for making the process seamless and easy. Many more thanks to everyone else, but especially Jim Howard, Bethany Marshall, and Nickcole Watkins.

I also want to thank and acknowledge the inspiration and example of all parents who truly care about their children and want the best for them.

ABOUT THE AUTHOR

Daniel Kingston trans- forms people's lives through coaching and teaching the family dynamic. He partners with the Family Success Insti- tute to create and share effec- tive strategies and techniques to bring true joy, fulfilment, and happiness to families and their children.

Daniel creates thriving family environments through individual consulting and live training. He currently works with couples, teenagers, and parents. He has degrees in engineering and business, and has worked as a business consultant where he turned companies around from near bankruptcy to profitable and sustainable in a short time.

When Daniel started his young family, he realized there is a lot to learn in being a great parent. Daniel begin interviewing parents and researching to discover what make families succeed and he committed to helping his family (and those around him) anyway that he could. He found that his business knowledge and the techniques gathered from others worked together to create effective family management tools and protocols.

Daniel has coached struggling couples to find love again, and anxious teenagers to find a compelling purpose in life and engage with life, as well as helping individuals create a compelling and rewarding family life.

Daniel has partnered with Family Success Institute to create this book because he knows all success begins at home and he is committed to helping families find it for themselves. He lives with his family and enjoys the great outdoors in Utah.

Website: https://www.familysuccessinst.com
Email: familysuccess@familysuccessinst.com
Facebook: www.facebook.com/familysuccessinstitute

Thank You

Still need a little help getting there with your family?

I've learned through the years that people don't usually go to Home Depot to proactively buy sheetrock. They go to Home Depot because they need to patch a hole in their wall. It's a reactive purchase.

In much the same way, most families don't plan and implement a life success strategy for their infant or child. Most families don't plan or implement how to build character in their children. And there are very few manuals of how to do it anyway.

Most parents do the best they can with what they have and know. I wish they understood how important it is to be proactive in their parenting and their long-term family experience, but too often they wait until there is a crisis or serious family problem that often changes the entire course of your child's or family's lives.

What if it could have been avoided?

Family Success Institute patches the holes. More importantly, we prevent the damage in the first place along with sprucing up all areas of the house.

As a way to say thank you to our readers, Family Success Institute has created a gift for you to get you started on your journey or to enhance the journey that is already underway.

Download the sample (and editable) Command Center Chart and Checklists at http://familysuccessinst.com/freedownloads

And let us know what you think! We love hearing from our readers.

Family Success Institute Team
familysupport@familysuccessinst.com
FB: www.facebook.com/familysuccessinstitute

Printed in the USA
CPSIA information can be obtained
at www.ICGtesting.com
JSHW021956150824
68134JS00055B/1964